Representations, Targets, and Attitudes

Representation and Mind
Hilary Putnam and Ned Block, editors

Representations, Targets, and Attitudes

Robert Cummins

A Bradford Book
The MIT Press
Cambridge, Massachusetts
London, England

This book was set in Palatino by Asco Trade Typesetting Ltd., Hong Kong and was printed and bound in the United States of America. This book was printed on recycled paper.

Library of Congress Cataloging-in-Publication Data

Cummins, Robert.
  Representations, targets, and attitudes / Robert Cummins.
    p.   cm.—(Representation and mind)
  "A Bradford book."
  Includes bibliographical references and index.
  ISBN 0-262–03235-X (hc : alk. paper)
  1. Representation (Philosophy) 2. Mental representation.
I. Title. II. Series.
B105.R4C84   1996
128'.2—dc20
                                    95-22502
                                       CIP

Contents

Acknowledgments

Substantial portions of this book have been presented to various audiences around North America, all of whom have contributed friendly suggestions as well as criticism. I have also had feedback from two graduate seminars at the University of Arizona, as well as from two National Endowment for the Humanities (NEH) summer seminars for college teachers. I have discussed various aspects of the theory endlessly with my colleague and friend Chris Maloney, who surely deserves as much credit for his patience as for his considerable insight. Most of all, I owe a huge debt to my wife, Denise Dellarosa Cummins, who is my constant reality check when doing the philosophy of mind and psychology. There is nothing like having a first-rate in-house cognitive psychologist to keep a philosopher from engaging in parlor game philosophy. And there is nothing like having constant encouragement from someone whose reaction to the material really matters.

Substantial chunks of an article I wrote many years ago, "Intention, Meaning and Truth Conditions," have been incorporated into chapter 10. Thanks to *Philosophical Studies* for allowing me to use that material here. Finally, thanks go to Laleh Quinn who did a lot of the dirty work in addition to providing philosophical feedback.

John Haugeland told me to take my time with this book and get it right. Well, John, I took a lot of time, but I fear a lot of it was spent on my horses and with Masha and Katya who we brought home from Russia a year ago. So I probably didn't get it right. I absolve you, and all the others who helped, of any responsibility for what may turn out to have been a loony idea.

Representations, Targets, and Attitudes

Chapter 1
Introduction

Contemporary theories of cognition make heavy use of the concept of mental representations. These theories all share the view that cognizing is processing mental representations. As a result, *the* topic in the philosophy of mind for some time now has been to explain the relevant notion of mental representation—to say, in some illuminating way, what it is for something in the mind to represent something. We can put this problem in perspective by comparing it to other problems that arise in connection with mental representation.

The Problem of Mental Representation

The difficulties surrounding mental representation can be ranged under four heads:

1. *Content:* Which contents are represented in the mind? What information is actually represented in the mind when it goes about its cognitive business?
2. *Form:* What form does mental representation take? There is the very general issue of what kind or kinds or representational scheme or schemes the mind employs (e.g., images, symbolic structures, activation vectors), and there are many particular issues concerning which of the available forms within a given scheme are employed in a given task.
3. *Implementation:* How are the mind's representational schemes implemented in the brain?
4. *Definition:* What is it for one thing to represent another?

The first three problems are, in various degrees, problems for empirical research. The fourth is a philosophical problem. But, in spite of this (rather artificial) division between empirical science and philosophy, answers to any one of the four questions constrains answers to the others. Answers to (1) and (2) are mutually constraining because a given content may be representable in one scheme but not in another, or because a given content may be represented efficiently in one scheme, and not in another. Answers to (2) and (3) are mutually constraining because some representational schemes may not have neural implementations, or may not have neural representations in our brains. And the first three issues evidently constrain the issue of definition, for a good definition of representation should be compatible with the contents, forms, and implementations that mental representations are known to take.

Since our problem in this book is going to be the problem of definition, it is worth taking explicit notice of the way in which (1) through (3) constrain (4).

As I see it, the most fundamental substantive constraints on a philosophical theory of mental representation (i.e, on a definition) are these:

- *Explanatory Constraint:* The theory should underwrite the explanatory appeals that cognitive theory makes to mental representation.
- *Implementation Constraint:* The theory should be compatible with the best scientific stories about what sorts of things actually do the representing in the mind/brain.

There are several representationalist theories of cognition currently on offer, of course. The possibility is very much open that different theories give rise to different explanatory and realization constraints. It is supposed by many, for example, that connectionist architectures place special constraints on both the kinds of representational schemes that are possible (no language of thought), and on the explanatory role played by representation (computation, being local, is not defined over the representations, which are distributed) (Smolensky, 1987; Fodor and Pylyshyn, 1988; Fodor and McLaughlin, 1990). A single, unified theory of mental representation might, therefore, be impossible. Perhaps science will settle on one approach to cognition eventually, but this seems unlikely to happen in the near future. Meanwhile, we shall just have to limp along with what we have, keeping in mind that our efforts may all be obsolete one day, just like the science on which they are parasitic.

Notice that among my fundamental constraints on a theory of representation, one does *not* find a constraint to the effect that a theory of mental representation should explain ordinary content attributions, such as "Peter believes the Normans invaded England in 1066." It would be nice to know what beliefs and desires are, and what it is to believe or desire that *p* rather than *q*. I will, in fact, have something to say about this. But the problem of mental representation, as I see it, is not primarily the problem of explaining the kind of content attributions that figure in ordinary attitude talk. The reasons for this will emerge as we go along, but it is well to be forewarned.

Naturalizing Content
A good deal of the recent philosophical literature on mental representation takes the problem to be one of naturalizing content. The motivation here is ontological: one wants representation defined in a way that makes it clear that the representation relation is, unlike demonic possession or spell-casting, a naturalistic relation of the sort countenanced by contemporary science. In practice, the operative constraint is that representation should be defined in a way that avoids the use of semantic terms such as 'means', 'refers', 'true', and also avoids intentional terms such as 'believes', 'desires', and 'intends'.

My ontological conscience is pretty weak. I'm no substance dualist, but I find propositions, possible worlds, numbers, and sets unavoidable. Since I have no idea how to be a hard-headed ontological physicalist about these, I feel uncomfortable about banging the table over the ontological status of representation. However, I do think that the standard practice of insisting on a definition in nonsemantic and nonintentional terms is quite proper on methodological grounds. A definition of representation in semantic terms would simply be circular. The term 'representation' is just a generic semantic term. If we don't avoid other semantic terms in its definition, we have no very good reason to suppose the definition makes any worthwhile intellectual progress.

The stricture against intentional terms requires a bit more comment. I think the general idea is that "*t* is a thought *that p*" involves a relation between *t* and the proposition *that p* that is mysterious in just the same way as the relation between a representation and what it represents: a meaning relation of some sort. On many accounts (e.g., Fodor, 1975, 1987), thinking *that p* requires representing the proposition *that p*. On almost every account, including my own, thinking *that p* requires representing something, though it may not require representing the proposition *that p*. If any of these accounts of thought are on the right track, defining representation in terms of thought would be regressive at best, and that is enough to motivate the stricture against intentional terms in the definition of representation. But there is a more general reason as well. Current cognitive science typically seeks to explain cognition by appeal to representation. This explanatory strategy is undermined if representation cannot be defined in a way that makes it independent of cognition. For example, a definition of representation in terms of rationality or inference (Dennett, 1987; Pollock, 1989) evidently threatens to undermine the standard explanatory strategy. By the same token, the capacity to think, believe, intend, plan, and desire is a cognitive achievement that is, or presupposes, the very sorts of phenomena that appeals to the processing of representation are supposed to explain. It is commonly held that only (at least minimally) rational creatures can be said to have beliefs or plans (e.g., Pollock, 1989). We do not want to explain belief in terms of rationality, rationality in terms of representation, and representation in terms of belief.

The upshot is that the widespread idea that representation should be defined nonsemantically and nonintentionally is a corollary of what I called the *explanatory constraint* above. *Representation* is an explanatory primitive in a science that seeks to explain mental phenomena generally, and cognitive phenomena in particular. We do the foundations of this science no service, then, if we define representation in mental or cognitive terms.

A final word needs to be said about prerequisites: I m going to assume familiarity with the recent philosophical literature on mental representation. This is not intended as a text. In the same spirit, though with less confidence, I am going to assume passing familiarity with contemporary cognitive science. This seems fair enough: philosophers of physics assume familiarity with physics, so philosophers of cognitive science ought to be able to make the analogous assumption. There is a regrettably widespread assumption in philosophy that one can be a philosopher of mind without knowing what science has to tell us about the mind. We seem to have got over that sort of a prioristic isolationism in the rest of the philosophy of science (though I suspect some philosophy of language still goes on in splendid isolation from linguistics); it s time we got over it in the philosophy of mind. The idea that the philosophy of mind generally, and the theory of content in particular, is a branch of the philosophy of science, is not exactly universal. Perhaps it is contentious. So be it. I just can't imagine what else a respectable philosophy of mind could *be*.

Chapter 2
Contents and Targets; Attitudes and Applications

Beginning with Error

Theories of mental representation are frequently criticized for a failure to do justice to *mis*representation. Consider causal theories: According to causal theories, a typical case of *mis*representation is a case in which a horse causes a |cow|[1] rather than a |horse|. But if a horse causes a representation, then that representation cannot be a |cow|, since it isn't caused by a cow. Perhaps the representation in question is a |cow or horse|. But then it isn't a misrepresentation of a horse as a cow after all. There are cures proposed in the literature for this problem (dubbed the disjunction problem by Fodor), and for analogous problems that arise in connection with other theories of mental representation, but they are rather *precious*, hence not really convincing. There is more to good philosophy than being able to rebut the counterexamples.

Rather than begin with a theory of representation and then see whether it allows a coherent account of error, I propose to begin with a theory of error in the hope that this will place some useful constraints on further theorizing about representation. This may amount to little more than squeezing the balloon in a different place: one might pessimistically predict that it is bound to bulge *somewhere*. Still, a *new* bulge would be welcome. I'm tired of the disjunction problem.

Targets and Contents

Suppose Σ is a chess machine. It uses a matrix, POS(row, col), to represent board positions. Σ is engaged in an endgame. The current position is P1 (figure 2.1), so

$$POS(1, 7) = k,$$

$$POS(2, 6) = B,$$

1. A |cow| is a mental representation whose content is (roughly) the same as the word "cow."

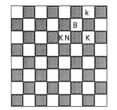
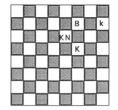
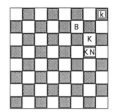

P1: the starting position   P2: the position after M   P3: the position R_{P3}
                                                                            actually represents

M=<k-kr1,   K-KB4,   k-kr2>

	1	2	3	4	5	6	7	8
1							k	
2						B		
3			KN		K			
4								
5								
6								
7								
8								

	1	2	3	4	5	6	7	8
1								
2						B	k	
3				KN				
4					K			
5								
6								
7								
8								

	1	2	3	4	5	6	7	8
1								k
2						B		
3						K		
4						KN		
5								
6								
7								
8								

R_{P1}: the representation R_{P2}: the representation R_{P3}: a representation of
      of the starting   of P2, the positon after M   P3, the representation
      position Σ constructs to
                                                                                        representP2

Figure 2.1
Chessboards and their representations.

$$POS(3,5) = KN,$$

$$POS(3,7) = K,$$

and POS(row, col) is 0 for every other value of row and col. A subroutine,
LOOK-AHEAD, anticipates k-kr1. To prevent stalemate, it investigates K-
KB5, and anticipates k-kr2. Call this series of possible moves M. LOOK-
AHEAD requires a representation of the position after M, viz. of P2. It
requires R_{P2}. Suppose what it actually constructs, however, is R_{P3}, which
represents P3, not P2. Since P3 is a stalemate, LOOK-AHEAD concludes
that M leads to stalemate and rejects K-KB5 as a response to k-kr1.

Σ's tokening of R_{P3} in this situation is error. What makes it error is the
fact that there is a mismatch between the state of affairs Σ needs to represent when it tokens R_{P3}, namely P2, and the state of affairs R_{P3} actually
represents, namely P3. Call the former Σ's *target* in tokening R_{P3} on this
occasion. Call whatever is specified by R_{P3}'s satisfaction condition—the
condition that says that R_{P3} is satisfied by P3—its *content*. Then *tokening a
representation is error when the target of tokening it on that occasion fails to
satisfy its content*.

What makes P2 Σ's target in tokening R_{P3}? In the example, Σ constructs a particular data structure—the matrix R_{P3}—at a given point in the computation. What the computation "requires" at that point is R_{P2}, a data structure that represents the position P2, the position after M. That is, as it were, what Σ is trying to represent when it constructs R_{P3}, and that is what Σ proceeds to use that data structure to represent. Representing the position after M—P2 in this case—is, in short, the function of tokening R_{P3} on the occasion in question, even though, of course, R_{P3} does not represent P2 but P3.

The notion of a representational target is essentially a functional notion, then. When we say that the computation *requires* a data structure that represents the position after M, what we mean is that the function of tokening R (on that occasion) is to represent T. This formulation reflects the idea that we can explain *why Σ tokens R on a particular occasion* by appeal to the fact that T is R's target. For example, Σ tokens R_{P3} in order to represent the board position after M, something it does in order to compute its next move. Note, however, that an appeal to R's target does not explain why Σ tokens a representation with a particular content. In the example, Σ tokens R_{P3} in order to represent the position after M. R_{P3} does not represent the position after M, however, but P3 instead. To explain why, in this situation, Σ tokens a representation of P3, we need to investigate the actual computational history of Σ's production of R_{P3} on the occasion in question.

Targets, then, are determined by the representational function of tokening a representation on a particular occasion in a particular context, not by the content of the representation tokened. In our example, the target on the occasion in question is P2 regardless of what representation is tokened or what the content of that representation is. It is precisely the independence of targets from contents that makes error possible. If the content of a representation determined its target, or if targets determined contents, there could be no mismatch between target and content, hence no error. Error lives in the gap between target and content, a gap that exists only if targets and contents can vary independently. It is precisely the failure to allow for these two factors[2] that has made misrepresentation the Achilles heel of current theories of representation.

---

2. "Two factors": the target-content distinction should not be confused with the two factors in so-called two-factor theories (e.g., Block, 1986). The two factors of two-factor theories—typically conceptual role on the one hand and some causal or historical connection to the environment on the other—are designed to capture the distinction between narrow and wide content, not the distinction between correctness and error. A mismatch between narrow and wide content, for example, between water as colorless potable liquid and water as H_2O, or between brisket as breast of beef and brisket as breast of beast, is precisely NOT error, as Burge (1979), for example, is at pains to argue.

The obvious way to think of representational error, as Jerry Fodor once said to me in conversation, is this: Error occurs when a representation is *applied to* something it is not *true of*, for example, when one applies a representation of a horse to a cow. The distinction in this formulation between what a representation is *applied to* and what it is *true of* is precisely the distinction between a representation's target and its content. The crucial point is that what determines what a representation is *true of* must be independent of what determines what it is *applied to*, otherwise error is problematic. It follows from this that a theory of representational content—a theory that says what it is for R to be *true of* T—is only part of the story about representation. We require, in addition, a theory of target fixation, a theory that says what it is for R to be *applied to* T. Since the target of tokening a representation is, as it were, the thing the representation is intended to represent, I shall say that representations *mean* (or *represent*) their contents, but that a use of a representation *intends* its target. *Intentionality* is thus different from *meaning*; the former is part of the theory of targets, while the latter is part of the theory of representational content. Using this terminology, we can say that representational error occurs when there is a mismatch between what a representation means and what its use intends. The *intentional content* of r is therefore not the actual content of r at all, but, rather, the *intended* content of some use of r.

"Intend" is a technical term here. I do not, of course, suppose that cognitive systems generally intend their targets consciously, that is, that whenever t is the target of a use of r in Σ, Σ forms the intention to use r to represent t. But I do think the technical sense is a natural extension of this usual sense. In the case of conscious, deliberate use, intended content is quite literally the content one intends to represent. As always, one may not succeed in doing what one intends, hence one may fail to represent what one intends to represent. We will see shortly that the failure to distinguish intentional content (= target) from meaning (= representational content) derives from the fact that they are conflated in *attitude content*.

How do targets, that is, representational functions or intentional contents, get fixed? There will be an extended discussion of this question in a later chapter. For now, some rough indications and a few examples will, hopefully, suffice to give the idea. Think of cognitive systems as incorporating mechanisms whose function is to represent certain things. For example, the function of a simple visual system might be to represent the local spatial layout—the relative sizes, shapes, and distances of objects from one another and from the observer. When this mechanism constructs a representation, the target of the representation it constructs is the cur-

rent local spatial layout, whatever that happens to be. So the representational function of the mechanism, together with the current state of the
world, determines what the current target is. I call mechanisms like this—
mechanisms with specified representational functions—*intenders*, for the
mind's contribution to intentional content, that is, to target fixation, is determined by the representational functions of such mechanisms. Perceptual systems are intenders in this sense, and they have more primitive
intenders as components. The visual system, for example, might have intenders whose business is to represent corners or edges.

Simple (i.e., single-function) programming variables provide a transparent illustration of how targets get fixed in a computational system. A
chess program might have a variable CURRENT_POSITION. Binding a
value to that variable amounts to aiming a representation at the current
position, because the program's logical design embodies the assumption
that evaluations of that variable amount to looking up the current position. That is why we name the variable the way we do: We name variables after targets. The mechanism that constructs representations and
binds them to CURRENT_POSITION is an intender: Anything whose
function it is to bind representations to CURRENT_POSITION is an
intender whose target is the current position. The "world," of course,
determines (if anything does) what the current position actually is. So, as
with the visual system lately imagined, the actual target of a particular use
of a representation is determined by the representational function of the
intender that tokens it together with the state of the world.

Evaluating CURRENT_POSITION amounts to looking up the current
position regardless of what CURRENT_POSITION is actually bound to,
that is, regardless of what the representation stored in CURRENT_POSI-
TION actually represents. We can have error, and its characteristic consequences, precisely because CURRENT_POSITION can be bound to a
value that does not represent the current position. The system will take
the value of CURRENT_POSITION to be the current position, and, in
that sense, the representation bound to CURRENT_POSITION could be
said to represent the current position *to the system*, whether or not that
representation is actually satisfied by the current position. There is a way
of hearing the difference between "what R represents *to the system*," and
"what R *actually* represents," as the distinction between target and content. But this is a dangerous way of thinking about the target-content distinction, because it tends to conflate it with the distinction between what
a representation means *to Σ* and what it means *to us*. This latter distinction is not the target-content distinction, but the distinction between the
content R has in Σ's representational scheme and the content it has in
ours.

Intenders, then, not the representations in them, determine targets.[3] Indeed, given the way I have introduced intenders, saying that intenders determine targets is equivalent to saying that the target of tokening R is determined by the representational function of tokening R. A consequence of this is that representations are not, in themselves, erroneous. The same representation can be error in one intender (or in one intention, as we might say), but not in another. Consider Pavlov's dog Rover, conditioned to expect food, hence salivate, on hearing a bell. Hearing a bell reliably causes Rover to token a |food|, but this is not error because the |food| in question is tokened by an intender whose function is to represent the expected-stimulus. If hearing a bell were to cause an intender whose function is to represent the current auditory stimulus to token a |food|, *that* would be error.[4]

3. In earlier drafts of this manuscript, and in Cummins (1992), I used the term "BOX" for what I am now calling intenders. That use of the term "BOX" engendered a good deal of confusion because I wrongly introduced it as an adaptation of Schiffer's use of the term (1987). Schiffer's boxes are distinguished by cognitive function rather than by representational function, as intenders are. As Schiffer thinks of the matter, the belief box and the goal box are distinguished by such facts as this: The representations in the belief box are susceptible to retraction if undercut or rebutted by a defeater (Pollock, 1986), whereas, as every planner knows, a representation in the goal box should be retracted when the same representation appears in the belief box. What I am now calling intenders are distinguished by representational function. 'Belief' and 'desire' do not name intenders at all, not even very abstract ones, as I wrongly suggested in the works cited.

The ideas underlying Schiffer's boxes and my intenders are thus quite different. Schiffer wants to represent the difference between two different kinds of attitudes one can take to a proposition, that is, the difference between believing p and desiring p, the enabling assumption being the functionalist idea that this difference is a difference between two different ways of processing representations. I want to represent the difference between aiming r at t and aiming r at t^*. If that is what you are after, belief and desire boxes are non-starters, because the difference between belief and desire is not a difference in what you intend to represent, but a difference in what the system is going to do with the implicated representations whatever they are intended to represent.

4. The theory advocated here has the same form as that advocated by Dretske in "Misrepresentation" (1986). Dretske's formulation is this:

> d's being G means$_f$ that w is $F =_{df} d$'s function is to indicate the condition of w, and the way it performs this function is, in part, by indicating that w is F by its (d's) being G.

This formulation creates a place for error to live, viz. in the gap between what something actually indicates and what is its function to indicate—its target, in effect. But note that what it defines is not the content of d's being G, but the *target* of d's being G. Or rather, it would define the target of d's being G but for two factors. (1) The definition is in terms of indication rather than representation, whereas the function of most representations is not to indicate, as I shall argue in a later chapter. (2) The definition is evidently intended to apply to a representational type: the function of d's being G is to indicate, that is, to covary with, w's being F, and this makes sense only as applied to types, and it is tokens, not types, that have targets.

Falsehood and Error

It is tempting to think of misrepresentation as a case of representing falsely. We think of a system confronted with a cow and tokening a |horse|. That, surely, is a case of misrepresenting a cow as a horse. And that, in turn, is surely just representing a cow as a horse, that is, falsely representing something as something it isn't. It looks as if misrepresenting x is representing x, but falsely. The "mis" can just be dropped; it is not doing any work.

But this is a confusion of misrepresentation and falsehood. Once we see that targets are determined by intenders and not by the representations they token, we are in a position to see that error is distinct from falsehood. Suppose Σ tokens r when it needs to represent x as F, but that r represents x as G. This is error even if x *really is* G, so falsehood is not a necessary condition of error. Moreover, failing to represent x as F when x's being F is the target is error even if x *is not* F. Where is it written that a system needs only to represent the facts? Often—in hypothetical reasoning, for example—Σ will need to represent x as F even though x is not F. Falsehood in the goal box is normal; tokening truths in the goal box is a kind of pathology.

The point generalizes from truth to satisfaction. Most representations don't have propositions as contents, hence aren't the sorts of things that could be true or false anyway. R_{P3}, for example, represents a board position; it has a satisfaction condition, not a truth condition. What determines whether a representation like R_{P3} is error, however, is not whether there is some actual state of affairs that satisfies it, but whether it is satisfied by its target, which may not be an actual state of affairs. A target is determined by the function of tokening a representation on a particular occasion, in a particular context. Representational types, therefore, don't have targets, only tokens have them: they inherit them from the intenders that create them. Thus, a representation's content (its satisfaction condition), which attaches to the type, together with the state of the world, is not enough to determine whether or not tokening that representation is error. We need, in addition, to know the target of tokening the representation—what the representation is applied to—and that is determined by what intender has tokened it, that is, by the representational function of tokening the representation on the occasion and in the context in question.[5]

---

5. Of course, the content of a representational type, together with the state of the world, is not enough to determine truth value or satisfaction either, if there are, for example, indexicals in the representation. The present point is that fixing truth value or satisfaction won't determine whether there is error, since (1) some targets aren't actual, and (2) matching an actual object or state of affairs that is not the target is still error.

Since error isn't the same as falsehood, it follows that truth isn't the opposite of error. Indeed, truths are error when the targets are falsehoods, for example, when the target is a supposition in a reductio proof. Representations are often tokened to represent some particular false proposition, or to represent something that is not actual. Equally important is the fact that a representation of the proposition that p will be error when the target is the proposition that q, regardless of the truth values of p and q.

An embarrassing consequence of the fact that truth is not the opposite of error is the realization that we *have* no word for the opposite of error. I propose to call it *correctness*. A representation has been correctly applied when it hits its target. If r represents a proposition, then an application of r is correct if it hits the target proposition (assuming the target is a proposition). Since the target proposition can be a false proposition, the question of whether r is correctly applied is orthogonal to the question of whether it is true. If r represents an object or property, then an application of r is correct if it is satisfied by the target object or property. Since targets need not be actual, correctness is orthogonal to satisfaction by something in the real world.

Illustration of the Distinction between Falsehood and Error
There is, as I remarked at the beginning of this section, a temptation to think that we can do without the distinction between target and content because we are used to thinking of erroneous representation as false representation. For instance, we think of information stored in the mind in what psychologists call propositional form, that is, as sentences in the language of thought. Imagine a bit of stored knowledge:

1. Letters are more easily recognized in the context of words than alone.
2. In chess, one should develop the queen early.

We notice that (1) is true, whereas (2) is false, and this seems to be all there is to the issue of representational error: if we could explain where truth conditions come from, we could explain error: an erroneous representation is simply one that has an unsatisfied truth/satisfaction condition.

But this will not do. Consider (1). Letters are also more easily recognized in the context of pronounceable nonwords. Call the set of words and pronounceable nonwords the superwords. Then (3) is also true:

3. Letters are more easily recognized in the context of superwords than alone.

Imagine that a student is taught both (1) and (3) but stores only (1). Faced with a choice between (1) and (3) in a multiple-choice examination in which the question is, "Which of the following best describes the word-superiority effect?," a student retrieves (1), yielding a wrong answer. Proposition 1, while true, is a misrepresentation of the target. It is error in spite of being true because its target is not simply The True, or a truth about letter recognition, but a particular truth about letter recognition. Thus, the truth conditions of (1) do not suffice to determine whether its "activation" or use on a particular occasion is error or not.

We can trace the error just imagined to the difference between "words" and "superwords". When (1) was stored, what was needed was an expression denoting the class of superwords, but what it "wrote" was an expression denoting the class of words. When (1) was constructed, the expression "words" was an error because the target of that expression, at the time it was constructed and stored, was the class of superwords, not the class of words. The case of terms, as opposed to sentences, makes it clear that a theory of truth and satisfaction conditions cannot provide a theory of error. Knowing the satisfaction conditions for "words" in (1) does not, and could not, tell us whether "words" in (1) is error. In addition to knowing which class of things actually satisfies "words," we need to know which class of things is the target of "words" in (1), and this, as we have seen, does not reduce to knowing whether (1) is true.

Representations, Applications, and Attitudes

Call an intender whose function is to represent t a t-intender. When a t-intender tokens a representation r, I call the result an *application* of r to t. For example, when the position-after-M intender tokens R_{P3}, we have an application to the effect that the position after M is P3. But the content of R_{P3} is not *that the position after M is P3*. To see this, we have only to note that when the current-position intender tokens the same representation, the result is an application with a different content, viz. *that the current position is P3*. R_{P3}, by itself, simply represents P3. This example shows that a system's applications can have contents distinct from the contents of its representations. In fact, the example shows more than this: the example shows that a system's applications can have contents distinct from the contents of *any* of its representations, for we may suppose that Σ is incapable of constructing a representation—an explicit data structure—whose content is *that the position after M is P3*. In general, then, one cannot infer that there is a representation with the content C from the fact that there is an application with the content C. When the position-after-M intender tokens R_{P3}, the result is a propositional application, but it is a propositional application that does not involve the explicit representation of any proposition.

We are now in a position to see how applications relate to attitudes. Propositional attitudes such as belief, desire, and intention are treated by

Schiffer (1972), Fodor (1990b), and many others as cognitive (or computational or functional) relations to representations, that is, as representations with a characteristic cognitive function. Σ harbors the belief that p, on this conception, if a representation that p is in Σ's belief box. But once we have the distinction between representations and their applications before us, it is clear that attitudes should be treated as relations to applications, not as relations to representations. In the chess example, Σ believes *that the position after M is P3*. But Σ harbors no representation, in its belief box or anywhere else, with the content *that the position after M is P3*. The only representation in the picture is R_{P3}, a representation whose content is a certain position, not a proposition at all. The propositional content of the attitude—belief in this case—is the content of an *application* of R_{P3} to a certain target. When the position-after-M intender tokens R_{P3}, we get an application with the content *that the position after M is P3*, the content of the attitude.

Attitudes are distinguished in type—for example, belief is distinguished from desire—by cognitive function. Since it is applications, not representations, that are correct or incorrect, it is applications, not representations, that have cognitive functions of the sort that distinguish the attitude types. It makes sense to retract an application of r to t when a defeater (e.g., an application of $-r$ to t) is discovered, but it makes no sense to retract a representation. What could it mean to retract a representation? Eliminate it from one's representational scheme? (One decides that one will never use four-letter words, or never use sentences of the form, "The bottom line is . . ."). Evidently, the only relevant thing that could be meant by retracting a belief or desire is retracting an application of some representation, an application that is currently functioning as a belief or as a desire. Applications are the only kind of thing that can have the sort of functions that distinguish beliefs from desires.

An attitude is the result of giving a cognitive role to an application of a representation r to a target t. For example, a |bell| is applied to the target *current auditory stimulus* (|bell| $\supset$ *cas*), and the resulting application is put in the belief box.[6] The whole business might be implemented by

6. In Schiffer's language, a belief that p is an application with the content that p in the belief box. Applications, however, are not the sorts of things that are naturally thought of as things you could put in a box the way representations are. One can put a (token) word or sentence or picture in a box, but not an application of a word or sentence or picture. Of course, talk of putting something in a box is simply meant as shorthand for giving it a certain cognitive function. But the shorthand is not apt: Applications can certainly be given cognitive functions, but they can't be put in boxes because they are events or states, not objects. Representations can be put in boxes, but they cannot be given the sort of cognitive functions that characterize belief.

1. Binding |bell| to the variable *cas*.
2. Making this binding available to defeasible inference but not to goal specification.

Notice that this application (binding) is now available for processing even though the system nowhere has a representation whose content is the content of the application |bell| ⊃ *cas*. The content that the current auditory stimulus is a bell is available even though it is not represented, because (a) the variable *cas* is implemented as a storage location, and (b) the system's logical design is such that the representations bound to *cas* are taken to be representations of the current auditory stimulus. Not only can you have a representation with the content that the current auditory stimulus is a bell without representing that proposition, you can *store* the attitude for future use. Of course, you don't want to have the belief that the current auditory stimulus is a bell for very long. But you won't. The system will write over the |bell| in *t* when the *cas* changes.

Can we get a standing belief like the belief that Socrates was a Greek philosopher without representing the proposition that Socrates was a Greek philosopher? In principle, this is simple. Implement a properties-of-Socrates intender as a variable *pos* whose bindings the system takes to be properties of Socrates, and bind it to |philosopher| and |Greek|. It is pretty unlikely, of course, that a natural cognitive system would implement such an intender directly. I don't know what directly implemented intenders humans have, but a properties-of-Socrates intender is surely not one of them. This is an empirical issue, of course. I don't think anyone has any well-justified ideas about what representational resources it takes for a human mind to have the belief that Socrates was a Greek philosopher precisely because no one really knows what the innate intenders are or how they are organized. What we do know is that you cannot read the required representational resources off the content of the belief.

Once we see that we cannot move directly from the premise that there is an application with the content *c* to the conclusion that there is a representation with the content *c*, we can see the mistake in the widespread theory that the content of an attitude is inherited from the content of its constituent representation. According to this theory, which Fodor (1975, 1980) calls RTM (Representational Theory of Mind), an attitude with the content *c* is a relation to a representation with the content *c*. This theory, which I will call RTAC (Representational Theory of Attitude Content),[7]

---

7. Fodor calls this the Representational Theory of Mind. In *Meaning and Mental Representation* (1989), I called it the Representational Theory of Intentionality (RTI), for I was thinking of attitude content as intentional content, and distinguishing it from the contents of representations. I still want to preserve the distinction between attitude content and representa-

licenses the inference from "Σ believes that p" to "Σ represents that p," an inference the discussion above shows to be incorrect. From "Σ believes that p" we can infer that Σ harbors an application with the content that p. But from the fact that there is an application *that* p, we cannot infer that there is a representation *that* p, as the chess example demonstrates. The RTAC, in effect, conflates application content with representational content. The RTAC thus leaves no room for error, for, by identifying application content with represented content, it leaves no room for targets to be specified independently of represented contents, hence no room for a mismatch between target and represented content. If I cannot distinguish the content of R_{P3} from the content of the application that results when an intender tokens it, then I cannot distinguish the content of R_{P3} from its target, and so cannot allow for error.

We can sum all this up in a few simple principles:

• Attitudes are applications with a characteristic cognitive function. The semantic content of an attitude is thus the semantic content of its constituent application.

• Applications are the result of applying a representation to a target. The semantic content of an application is that the representation hits the target:

$$\text{Application content} = f(\text{represented content, target})$$

$$= f(\text{represented content, intentional content})$$

As we have seen, representations in themselves are not correct or incorrect, though they may be true or false, satisfied or not satisfied; only the application of a representation to some target can be correct or incorrect. And that is why applications, but not representations, can have cognitive functions of the sort that distinguish the attitudes from one another, and hence why attitudes inherit their contents from their constituent applications, not from the representations involved. The semantic function of a representation is to represent its content; the semantic function of an application is to hit its target. An application of a representation r to a target t always has the content that t is represented by r. For example, applying R_{P3} to the position after M has the content *that the position after M is P3*. An application of r to t is correct when the content of the *application* is true, that is, when r represents t, and an application of r

---

tional content, of course: The content of an attitude always goes beyond the content of its constituent representation. But I now wish to reserve "intentionality" for the relation a use of a representation in an attitude bears to its target. Representations *mean* their contents, and a use of a representation *intends* its target.

to *t* is error when the content of the application is false. This, I think, is what gives rise to the idea that the theory of representational error and correctness simply reduces to the theory of truth. In a sense, this is right: representational error and correctness can be defined, as we just did, in terms of the truth or falsity of applications. But, since the content of an application is never the same as the content of the representation applied, a theory that gives us truth conditions for applications does not gives us representational contents.

Nesting Intenders

Consider the chess example once again, and imagine, as we did earlier, that POSITION_AFTER_*M* is a programming variable. *M*, we may suppose, is itself a variable that gets bound to representations of move sequences. Since POSITION_AFTER_*M* cannot be evaluated if *M* is not bound, the *M*-intender, that is, the thing whose business is to represent the move sequence of current interest, is nested in the position-after-*m* intender. Since intenders can be nested, and since you get an application when an intender tokens a representation, you can get nested applications. For example, we get an application with the content *that* $<k$-*kr*1, *K*-*KB*5, *k*-*kr*2$>$ *is the sequence of current interest* nested in a application with the content *that the position after the sequence of current interest is P3*: you bind *M* to a representation of the sequence $<k$-*kr*1, *K*-*KB*5, *k*-*kr*2$>$, then bind POSITION_AFTER_*M* to R_{P3}.

The phenomenon of intender nesting shows how it is possible for there to be an unlimited number of targets: intender nesting makes a system's targets both systematic and productive in Fodor's sense (1975, 1987). In the lately imagined case of the multiple-choice examination, we assumed that the target of,

(1) |Letters are more easily recognized in the context of words than alone|,

was in fact,

(3) Letters are more easily recognized in the context of superwords than alone.

Proposition (3) is the target of (1) on the assumption that (1) is tokened by a mechanism whose function is to represent the best alternative in the current choice set, or something like it. Such targets are obviously not a permanent feature of the functional architecture of the mind. They are created on the fly, perhaps by binding a lot of variables. Binding a lot of nested variables is a vivid way of seeing that computational systems can generate a wealth of rather definite targets as processing progresses.

When thinking about targets, it is important to keep separate two ideas about what fixes them. One idea is that (1) the target of tokening r is what Σ *needs to represent* to succeed. The other is that (2) the target of tokening r is what Σ expects to find when r is accessed. The first makes target fixation epistemic, the second makes it a matter of architecture or design. It is the second idea that I want to endorse. It is easy to see why the epistemic conception is problematic: there may be no content such that, were Σ to represent it, Σ would succeed, for Σ's success or failure will depend on many things other than the use of a particular representation on a given occasion. Moreover, it is easy to imagine situations in which representing *t* would bring success, but for reasons unrelated to, or inappropriately related to, representing *t*. Σ may succeed *because* it wrongly rejects a move whose consequences are incorrectly represented. Adopting the epistemic conception of targets expressed in (1) will make it impossible to articulate such possibilities.

The conception of target fixation I want, then, is the conception expressed in (2), that the target of tokening r is what Σ expects to find when r is accessed. Not literally "expects" of course; the idea is that Σ incorporates a design assumption to the effect that a representation generated by a certain intender will be a representation of *t*. This is, as remarked above, the conception that falls naturally out of thinking of intenders as mechanisms for binding programming variables. Just as programs are designed around assumptions about what will be accessed when a given variable is evaluated, cognitive systems are designed around assumptions about what will be represented by various intenders. Specifying a system's design or functional architecture involves specifying what intenders are possible, and hence, on the current conception, what targets are possible. The targets that are possible for a given system are thus fixed by its functional architecture.[8]

Can Representations Determine Targets?

The central point of the theory of error proposed here is that targets are determined independently of representational contents. The question arises, therefore, as to whether a representation could somehow specify its own target.

In the abstract it seems clear that this cannot happen. *T* is the target of a given tokening of *R* just in case the function of that tokening of *R* is to

8. We will have occasion to qualify this in a later chapter, for, as mentioned earlier, there is often an indexical element to target fixation. That there is a current-position intender in Σ is fixed by its architecture. But what the current position is, and hence what a representation generated by the current-position intender must match to be correct, is determined by the world.

represent *t*. But the function of a given tokening of *R* is surely independent of the content of *R*. I don't mean to claim, of course, that the function of *tokening something with the content c* is independent of the content of *R*. Contents, no doubt, have functions, as Millikan (1984) has emphasized. But we must distinguish the function of a representational type—something that plausibly turns on its content—and the function of tokening it on a given occasion, which does not. The function of R_{P3} is, I suppose, to represent P3. But the function of its tokening by the current-position intender is to represent the current position, *whatever that is*. Since the current position need not be P3, it follows that the function of tokening R_{P3} cannot, in general, be the same as the function of R_{P3}.

But couldn't a representation say, in effect, "The Eiffel Tower is my target"? Certainly. But it won't follow that the target of this representation *is* the Eiffel Tower. Indeed, the fact that this representation says that its target is the Eiffel Tower will have no effect whatever on what its target actually is. To confirm this, we have only to remember that the representation in question could be generated by any number of different intenders. For example, an intender in the language-understanding system whose function is to represent the meaning of the current sentence might generate some such representation. Your language-understanding system did just that a moment ago. When it did, the target was not the Eiffel Tower but the meaning of the then current sentence, and the determination of that target was quite independent of the content of the representation you tokened.

Target and Referent

The fleeting temptation to suppose that the content of a representation could influence the target of some particular tokening of it derives from a tendency to conflate targets and referents (and, correlatively, content with sense): if you think targets are just referents, then, since a representation can specify its own referent, it seems it could specify its own target. Consider an |I am rich|: Isn't the target here the "speaker"?

To see what is wrong with this, imagine a context in which what I need is a representation of the proposition that Scrooge is rich, that is, a context in which my target is *that Scrooge is rich*. If what I produce on that occasion is an |I am rich|, we have representational error whether or not I am rich (provided I am not Scrooge, of course). The target of "I" need not be the speaker—that is its content. The target of "I" could be anyone or anything. That is what makes it possible for a tokening of "I" to be an error.[9] It is pretty obvious, on reflection, that targets are distinct from referents, for otherwise reference could not go wrong. Imagine a representation R whose referent is my right hand, and an intender L whose target is my left hand. When L generates R—the sort of thing one's visual system is liable to do when one is looking in a mirror—we have error. It is error precisely because there is a mismatch between referent and target. Satisfaction conditions—conditions that say, among other things, what refers to what—are contents, not targets.

It is easy to get confused about this if we are thinking about the content of an application rather than the content of a representation. The content of an application is, as we have seen, contributed in part by the intender. The possibility thus arises that the referent of an application is contributed by the intender. Since intenders determine targets, applications can refer to the targets of tokening their constituent representations. When R_{P3} (i.e., |P3|) is tokened by the current-position intender, the result is an application with the content *that the current position is P3*, that is, an application that is about the current position. Here, what the *application* is about—what it refers to, in one straightforward sense—is its target, viz. the current position, P1. But what the *representation* is about—*its* referent—is P3. Overlooking the distinction between the content of an application, and the content of its constituent representation, therefore, can lead to a conflation of the target of tokening R and R's referent.

Three Theories of Mental Content

We need, then, three distinct theories to deal with mental content:

1. A theory of representational content.
2. A theory of target fixation.
3. A theory of application content.

The *theory of representational content* must explain what it is for something to be a representation, and what it is for a given representation to have a particular content. A crucial constraint is that representational content should be distinct from application content and independent of target fixation.

The *theory of target fixation* must explain "the function of tokening a representation r is to represent t." A crucial constraint is that target fixation must be independent of representational content.

---

9. The content of an |I am rich| is, in any case, a proposition, not a person. When an |I am rich| is correctly applied, its target is the same as its content, viz. the proposition that I am rich. If we suppose that the target of an |I am rich| is the speaker, we are bound to get error, for then the content, being a proposition, has no chance of matching the target, a person.

Since the content of an application is a function of two factors, its target and its representation, the *theory of application content* must explain how target and representational content add up to the content of an application.

The problem of mental content is, then, three problems rather than one. Only by keeping these distinct is there any hope of emerging with a conception of mental representation that makes room for a robust conception of error.

Some Diagnostics

Why has the crucial concept of a target been neglected? Here, I think, is how it usually happens. One begins with an example such as, "Σ believes that the position after M is P3." That belief is error, one supposes, just in case it is false that the position after M is P3. Error in belief seems to be just the falsehood of a representation whose content is specified in the that-clause. One's theory of truth, then, will do as a theory of error. All that remains is to explain what it is for the belief to have the content *that the position after M is P3.*

The trouble starts when we consider an example divorced from any particular processing context. When Σ comes to believe that the position after M is P3, Σ is not simply in search of some truth or other, it is after the position after M. To get things right, Σ needs a very particular belief, a belief with the content that the position after M is P2. Realizing that another truth won't do is enough to show that a theory of truth won't do as a theory of error. One needs, at a minimum, to ask which truth the system is after on the occasion in question, and that is to ask after the target.

The minimum, however, isn't nearly enough. The story above moves immediately from the premise that Σ has a belief with the content *that the position after M is P3* to the conclusion that Σ harbors a representation with that content. Attention to the details of realization and processing reveals that this is a faulty inference. What Σ needs, on the occasion in question, is a representation of P2 targeted at the position after M. The only representation that enters the picture is R_{P3}, a representation of a position. We thus arrive at the distinction between the content of an application and the content of its constituent representation. Since beliefs with the same content can be differently constituted by different target plus representation combinations, and since targets are fixed by intenders, it follows that two beliefs with the same content can have different targets. When the contents-of-the-basket intender generates a representation of the cat, you get a belief with the content that the cat is in the basket, but the target is the contents of the basket. When the location-of-the-cat intender generates a representation of the basket, you get a belief with the content that the cat is in the basket, but the target is the location of the cat. The conditions for error are, therefore, very different. A representation of the cat, however excellent, is error in the latter case, while a representation of the basket is error in the former.

At least as serious as ignoring the details of processing and realization is the obsession with belief to the exclusion of the other attitudes. Truth is evidently not typically a necessary condition of correctness in intention or desire, and this obvious fact should have been enough to generate a distinction between error and falsehood. Unfortunately, it is all too easy to drop the ball by supposing that a correct intention or desire is simply a rational intention or desire, and ship the problem off to epistemologists without noticing that the subject has been changed from representational error to inferential error.[10] Since inference is something philosophy is used to understanding in terms of truth, it might seem that error in intention and desire really introduces nothing new.

The bottom line is that you cannot hope to do justice to mental content by thinking about the truth conditions of belief attributions. The philosophy of psychology isn't the semantics of folk-psychological locutions. To certain philosophers of mind this may seem like an unemployment opportunity. But, after all, it really never was in the cards to get a theory of mental content out of a semantics of English belief sentences (Cummins, 1991a).

---

10. This is a change of subject that conceptual role semanticists are bound not to notice, as we will see in a later chapter. Since conceptual role semantics identifies R's content with R's epistemic liaisons, something with a "bad" content is just something involved in some bad inferences.

Chapter 3
More about Error

In this section, I distinguish two kinds of representational errors: "forced errors," which are unavoidable given the expressive power of the representational scheme, and "unforced errors," which are not due to any inadequacy in the scheme itself. Let's begin with some examples.

- No finite language, that is, no language with only finitely many expressions, is adequate to represent the facts of arithmetic.
- The Fahrenheit scale, being an interval scale, is inadequate to represent certain facts about temperature, namely ratios.
- Extensional logics appear to be inadequate to represent the logical form of subjunctive conditionals.
- Euclidean geometry has proved inadequate to represent the structure of physical space.
- People seem unable to see a human nose as concave rather than convex.
- Three-color schemes are not adequate to represent all possible territorial boundaries.

These are all cases of expressive inadequacy: a certain representational system just does not have the power to represent a certain domain. One of the things that makes such cases interesting is that they generate situations in which there is no right answer to the question of how to represent a given target. In general, there will not always be a best answer, or even a reasonably small set of best answers, and even when there is a best answer, it might not be very good. Borrowing a term from tennis, I call misrepresentations that arise from the expressive poverty of the representational scheme *forced errors*: forced errors are forced in that there is no possibility of a correct representation in such situations. The representational scheme simply lacks the requisite expressive power.

A central point about expressive adequacy is that it is a relation between a representational scheme and its target domain: an expressively adequate scheme is one that has the resources to "adequately represent" the domain that is its target. The relevant notion of adequacy here prob-ably cannot be made precise without sacrificing generality. Different kinds of schemes and domains may well call for different conceptions of adequacy: the inadequacy of extensional logic (if such it is) to represent the logical form of subjunctive conditionals is not obviously of a piece with the inadequacy of three-color schemes to represent boundaries. Haugeland (1990) may well be right in suggesting that different kinds of representational schemes represent different kinds of things. For example, it may be that there are things that can be represented iconically that cannot be represented symbolically and vice versa. If so, then there will be things a representational scheme cannot represent just because it is the kind of scheme it is. There is rich material for research here. Still, we seem to have a pretty good intuitive grasp of the idea that a representational scheme might or might not be up to the job of representing some spe-cified domain, and so I have little hesitation about taking this idea as primitive in the following discussion.

We have to be careful to distinguish the expressive power of a scheme of representation from the capacity of a particular system to use that scheme. English grammar allows for unlimited center-embedding, but human parsing architecture blows up at a depth of about 3, apparently be-cause of limitations on short term memory (Miller, 1956). Paul Smolensky (1987) has developed a scheme of distributed representation in connec-tionist networks that allows for the representation of complex hierarchical structures such as phrase markers, but until very recently (Smolensky, LeGendre, and Miyata, 1992) it was an open question to what extent connectionist processors could exploit the representational power thus achieved (Smolensky, 1994; Cummins, 1994). One of Galileo's most orig-inal ideas was to make the areas of Euclidian figures represent distances. Letting vertical lengths represent time, and horizontal lengths represent velocity, the area of a rectangle represents the distance traveled by a body moving with uniform velocity, and the area of a right triangle represents the distance traveled by a uniformly accelerated body. When acceleration isn't uniform, we get a right "triangle" with a curved hypotenuse. Here, the area represents the distance, but the standard straightedge and com-pass geometry of the day had no means of comparing the resulting area with others, and was therefore unable to exploit these representations.[1]

Forced error, then, arises when a system Σ uses a scheme R for repre-senting a domain T that R is not capable of representing. The situation is this: Σ makes a forced error in representing t as r when

---

1. The right curves could be produced accurately on the hypotenuse sides by tracing a conic section.

1. R is Σ's scheme for representing T.
2. Σ applies r (an element of R) to t.[2]
3. No element of R represents t.

At the point in the process where a representation of t is required, Σ is bound to use some element of R. But no element of R represents t, and so Σ's use of r to represent t is a forced error.

Not all representational error is forced, of course. People frequently misrecognize shrews and voles as mice. Sometimes, this is because they don't know about voles and shrews, so some of these errors might be forced errors. But even a zoologist who knows about voles and shrews might mistake a vole for a mouse on occasion, and this is an unforced error in that it is possible, so far as representational resources go, to avoid misrepresentation.[3]

Unforced errors are common. Logic students, asked to represent the logical form of, "I won't shoot unless he does," typically suggest "$H \supset I$" rather than "$I \supset H$" which is also in their repertoire. Illusions are typically unforced errors: It is not because we lack the representational resources to see it smaller that we see the full moon near the horizon much enlarged, nor does an afterimage, seen as a spot on a wall, appear to shrink when we approach the wall because we lack the capacity to represent the spot as constant in size (as the phenomenon of size constancy proves).

Unforced errors, then, differ from forced errors in that the scheme R that Σ uses to represent T actually can represent what needs to be represented. We get unforced representational error when Σ selects the wrong element of an adequate scheme.

1. Σ's scheme for representing T is R.
2. Σ applies r (an element of R) to t.
3. R contains an element that represents t, but r does not represent t.

Interesting empirical and theoretical questions can be seen to turn on whether certain errors are forced or unforced, or due to an inability to exploit an adequate scheme.

- Piagetians think a first-grader's errors on word arithmetic problems are forced errors; their opponents think they are unforced, due to mistakes in processing, not to expressive poverty (D. Cummins, 1988).

---

2. By an element of R, I mean a representation, whether simple or complex, that is part of the scheme R, a representation that is, as it were, well formed in R. This might be a picture, a diagram, a graph, a symbolic expression, an activation pattern, etc., depending on the scheme.
3. Even the zoologically untutored can have percepts of voles and shrews, of course, just as cameras can produce pictures that represent voles and shrews without having the corresponding concepts. But the capacity to perceptually represent a vole or shrew must be distinguished from the capacity to represent the property of being a vole or the property of being a shrew. Percepts, as Kant realized, are pointed at the *objects*, not the properties.

• Barring encapsulation, effects resting on unforced errors should be cognitively penetrable, whereas those resting on expressive inadequacy should not be.

• Learning, in the sense of improved performance, divides into three distinct kinds: (1) improvements in expressive power, (2) improvements in the capacity to exploit existing expressive power, and (3) improvements in inference (broadly construed) that reduce unforced errors.

• Expressively powerful schemes may be difficult to exploit, but weaker schemes may lead to forced errors which are difficult to correct because a new scheme amounts to an alteration in architecture.

Doubtless other issues would benefit from reconsideration in light of the distinction between forced and unforced errors, and the related distinction between the expressive power of a representational scheme and the power of a computational system to exploit it. But let us leave empirical theory to those whose errors are less likely to be forced, and focus instead on the implications for the theory of content.

Accuracy: Degrees of Correctness

Representational error and correctness often come in degrees. It is obvious on the face of it that some pictures, maps, and graphs are more accurate than others. For this reason, it is desirable to replace the categorical notion of correctness with the graded notion of *accuracy*.

Note that this move makes good sense only if we are careful to distinguish accuracy from truth and inaccuracy from falsehood. Graded notions of truth and falsehood are notoriously difficult to make coherent, yet everyone knows that some sentences, maps, graphs, and pictures are more accurate than others. We speak of getting closer to (or further from) the truth, yet this tends to degenerate into getting more (or fewer) truths in the face of the fact that a failure to express a truth is simply a falsehood (or nonsense). The solution to this paradox is to note that accuracy is a relation between representation and target, whereas truth is a relation between representation (or attitude) and fact. A representation r may be closer to the truth than r' because it is a more accurate representation of some truth than r'. This doesn't make r "more true" than r'; it simply makes it a more accurate representation of a target that happens to be a true proposition. I'll have more to say about accuracy in chapter 7. For now, I will simply take it for granted that representations can more or less accurately represent their targets.

Seriousness and Inaccuracy

The degree of error or inaccuracy should not be confused with its *seriousness*. The *seriousness* of an error depends on the extent to which the outcome of a process depends on accuracy. Representing mass as weight can give large errors that are not serious in certain cases, for example, in processes designed to determine only which of two nearby masses is the greater. On the other hand, very small errors can be very serious, as the annual death toll from mushroom poisoning testifies. Once we see that an error can be small but serious, or large but not serious, we see that what we might call the *effectiveness* of a representation (on a particular occasion or generally) is distinct from its accuracy. Even a perfectly accurate representation can fail to be effective because it is too costly to use.[4] Given limited space, a map that leaves out many features and distorts others may be more effective than a more accurate map that will fit in the available space (a single atlas page, say) only at the price of being unreadable. Approximations to a target (e.g., linear approximations to nonlinear functions) are often more effective because more tractable.

Given that it is, in a sense, effectiveness that matters, it is tempting to define correctness or accuracy in terms of effectiveness: A correct representation is one that is effective. This is the intuition that helps to drive conceptual role semantics (CRS) as well as adaptational role theories. But this intuition must be resisted. If we define accuracy in terms of effectiveness, we are left with no natural way to articulate the important point that the pursuit of accuracy is often too expensive to be an effective policy. This is just one aspect of a central theme of this book, viz. that use theories undermine the notion of error, and hence undermine the explanatory value of the concept of representational content. We require a clean distinction between accuracy and effectiveness if the concept of representation is to have the independent explanatory leverage that makes it an important primitive in cognitive science.

4. We must not confuse a situation in which a system is effective in spite of its errors with a system that makes effective errors.

Less accurate representations are often tolerable because they are less costly to compute. Misrepresenting a crow as a hawk is a less serious error for a field mouse than misrepresenting a hawk as a crow. Given that recognition must occur quickly, a fast but inaccurate system may be better than a slower more accurate one. Since crows greatly outnumber hawks, a fast system that generates many false-positive hawk identifications but no false negatives is less accurate but more effective than a slower system that generates fewer false positives while still avoiding false negatives.

Note, however, that this is not a remark about the relative effectiveness of crow and hawk representations, but of the relative effectiveness of two different recognitional systems. Given the presence of a crow, there is no reason to suppose that a |hawk| is the more effective representation. On the contrary: It will cause the mouse to lose time and energy.

Chapter 4
Use and Error

A central theme of this book is that the theory of representational content must abandon any form of the doctrine that meaning is use. I think *all* of the theories currently taken seriously are use theories of one kind or another. The only major contender that is self-consciously a use theory, however, is conceptual role semantics (CRS). If we want to see what is wrong with the idea that meaning is use, therefore, we do well to begin with CRS.

A word about "use". To use a representation is to apply it to a target. Uses, then, are simply applications. To specify how a representation is used on a particular occasion is to specify a particular target. To specify a general use of *r* ("how *r* is used") is to specify what targets *r* is (or can be) applied to. Use theories of meaning (representational content), then, take the meaning of a representation to be determined by what it is or can be applied to. The fundamental idea is simple: in a case of correct use, content = target. So if we know what a representation is applied to, and we know that the use is correct, we know the content. Use theories attempt to naturalize content by specifying a sufficient naturalistic condition under which use can be supposed to be correct. They then identify the content of *r* with whatever *r* is applied to when the specified correct use condition is satisfied. In chapter 5, we will see that causal theories are use theories in this sense, for they identify the content of *r* with its target when it is applied by a successful detector. Adaptational role theories are also use theories, for they identify the content of *r* with the target it was applied to in those cases that account for the replication of the applying mechanism (intender).[1]

---

1. As we will see in chapter 7, there is a "narrow" and a "wide" aspect to target fixation. We have, for example, an intender whose business it is to represent *the current board position* (narrow). But what the current board position happens to be on a given occasion will, of course, be determined by the world. A use theory of meaning gives you narrow contents if it identifies contents with (correctly hit) targets identified in terms of intender function; you get wide contents if it identifies contents with the (correctly hit) targets themselves.

It is a little trickier to see how CRS fits this template. CRS is what you get when you put functionalism about mental states together with the idea that some mental states are individuated by their contents: If functional role is what distinguishes mental states, and if believing that p is distinct from believing that q, then the difference between believing that p and believing that q must be a difference in functional role. Having come this far, the only issue remaining is what sorts of functional roles fix meaning.

The idea is to think of the meaning of a representation in a system Σ as fixed by the cognitive transitions it enables in Σ. This is analogous to the line empiricists took about the meaning of theoretical terms in science (Hempel, 1950). Just as empiricists wanted to identify the meaning of a theoretical term with the conceptual role it plays in its home theory, so CRS identifies the meaning of a mental representation with the conceptual role it plays in a kind of "automatic theory," namely a cognitive system.[2] We think of the functional roles that individuate contents as *conceptual* roles because we think of concepts as the things that make it possible for cognitive business to go forward. You cannot infer that McKinley is dead from the fact that he was assassinated if you don't have the concept of death. But if you cannot infer McKinley's death from his assassination, you do not seem to have the concept of assassination either. That, at any rate, is the intuition underlying CRS (Stich, 1983).

It is now pretty straightforward to see CRS as a use theory in the sense lately staked out. Use theories say that the meaning or r is determined by what Σ applies it to. What Σ applies r to will turn on what Σ believes (and its other attitudes), together with the stimuli that impinge on it and its computational architecture. These factors are just r's conceptual role in Σ. So conceptual role determines use, and use determines meaning.

CRS and Meaning-Incomparability

The Standard Objection to CRS is that systems that differ in their beliefs, or any other of their attitudes, will be *meaning-incomparable*: no mental

2. This, in fact, is just how computational theories of cognition were originally conceived. Linguistic competence, for instance, was to be explained on the hypothesis (1) that one had tacit knowledge of linguistic theory, and (2) that an automatic inference and control system applied the theory to produce and understand speech. If you hold a conceptual role theory of the meanings of the theoretical terms in linguistic theory, then it is natural to hold the same theory about the meanings of the terms of the tacit theory.

This little history lesson should give us pause. Conceptual role stories about the meanings of theoretical terms in science have been generally abandoned. It is hard to believe that what made CRS bad philosophy of science will somehow go away if we just put the theories in our heads.

representation in the one will mean the same as any mental representation in the other. Hence, systems that do not share *all* of their beliefs do not share *any*.

Here is how it is supposed to work. According to CRS, the meaning of a representation in a system Σ is determined by its conceptual role in Σ. One can picture conceptual roles (or functional roles, if you prefer) as follows. Each belief, desire, and so on, is a node in a connected graph, each connection representing what Fodor (1987) calls an epistemic liaison. The content of a given node is specified by its place in the rest of the graph. Adding or subtracting a node from the graph thus changes the meaning of every node. So, as threatened, systems that do not share *all* their beliefs do not share any.

An alternative route to the same conclusion goes like this. The content of a belief is given by its epistemic liaisons, that is, by all the evidential relations it bears to other attitudes (and perhaps other nonattitudinal states as well). Now, as Quine emphasized (1953), anything can be evidentially related to anything else via some connecting background theory. Hence, any difference in background theory will produce a difference in the epistemic liaisons that characterize a given belief.

It is generally thought that CRS can avoid this consequence only by invoking an analytic/synthetic distinction. If we allow only analytic connections in the graph that determines meaning, then meaning will be insensitive to mere differences in "collateral information" (Quine, 1960), for those differences do not effect analytic connections. There is, to be sure, a widespread intuition to the effect that one can have beliefs about arthritis even though one has some beliefs that turn out to be analytically false when construed as about arthritis (Burge, 1979). This intuition can certainly be challenged (Fodor, 1982), so the determined defender of CRS might feel reasonably safe if only a defensible analytic/synthetic distinction were on the cards. It is pretty widely conceded, however, that a defensible analytic/synthetic distinction is not on the cards, so CRS appears to be stuck with meaning-incomparability across persons and times. This line of argument is a central theme in Fodor and Lepore (1992).

It turns out, however, to be fairly easy to formulate CRS in a way that avoids the charge of meaning-incomparability. The new formulation does bring a kind of analytic/synthetic distinction in its train, but it is no more than what is already implicit in any computationalist theory that accepts the distinction between a system's attitudes on the one hand, and its fixed functional architecture on the other (Pylyshyn, 1984). It is arguable that connectionists do not have to accept this distinction (Schwarz, 1992), but few of those who have charged CRS with meaning-incomparability will be willing to take out connectionist insurance policies.

A Functionalist Version of CRS

The idea underlying CRS is that the meaning of a representation in a cognitive system is fixed by all the epistemic or evidential connections it enables, that is, by what Fodor calls its epistemic liaisons. The first thing to note when one comes to think about implementing this idea is that representations themselves do not enter into epistemic liaisons. Beliefs or desires or intentions can be justified or rational or warranted or probable on the evidence, and they can enter into making other propositional attitudes justified or warranted or rational or probable on the evidence. But a representation by itself can do none of these things. A representation, by itself, is *semantically* assessable but not epistemically assessable. My belief that war is hell may be justified by other beliefs, or by perceptual inputs, but my representation of war as hell, while it might be more or less adequate or accurate or useful, is not the sort of thing that could be justified or warranted.[3] Its contribution to the epistemic economy depends on what attitudes it enters into. A representation with the content *that I am rich* may enter into a rational desire or intention but an irrational belief. Representations thus determine epistemic liaisons only indirectly, via the attitudes they figure in.[4]

It is common, therefore, to find CRS formulated and discussed in a way that implies that it is attitudes, not representations, whose semantic content is determined by their epistemic liaisons. The initial idea is simply to identify an attitude's content with its epistemic liaisons. This view will entail that a belief *that p* and a desire *that p* do not have the same content, since a belief and a desire will never have the same epistemic liaisons. Indeed, they will typically have incompatible epistemic liaisons, since the desire that *p* typically has as an epistemic liaison the belief that not-*p*. This is hardly an unexpected consequence, though it is certainly not one advocates of CRS typically notice, let alone rush to embrace. If we want a CRS account of what it is for two attitudes to both be attitudes *that p*, we will require something more sophisticated than simply identifying content with epistemic liaisons. I propose to let this pass, since my real concern is with representational content, not attitude content.

The Formulation

Since representations affect epistemic liaisons only indirectly via the applications, and, through them, the attitudes they make possible, we need

---

3. Another way to put this is to say that only the *use* of a representation can be justified or warranted. This is why epistemological theories of meaning are inevitably use theories.
4. The same goes for applications. The same application can enter into different attitudes. Since instances of different attitude types are always characterized by different epistemic liaisons, it follows that epistemic liaisons alone will not give us the contents of applications.

to begin with a clear conception of the relation between representations and attitudes. Following Schiffer (1987) let's think of each attitude type as a kind of box—a belief box, a goal box, etc.—into which the system can put various applications. To get the belief that I am rich, my cognitive system puts an application with the content *that I am rich* in my belief box; to get the desire that I am rich, my cognitive system puts an application with the content *that I am rich* in my desire box.[5] I don't know how many kinds of boxes there are in a human cognitive system, or what they are, but that won't matter, because I propose to quantify over them in what follows. All that matters, then, is that there is a principled distinction between the representations a system uses, the representational uses it puts them to, and the cognitive functions of those uses.

Since it is attitudes that, in the first instance, have epistemic liaisons, let us begin by articulating a precise representation of the epistemic liaisons belonging to a given attitude. Begin with an A-state c_A, that is, cognitive state c that contains an attitude A. The set of paths in state space that intersect at c_A are the epistemic liaisons of A in the context of the state c_A, or A's conceptual role relative to c_A. But, of course, A can occur in others states as well. The conceptual role of A is just the set of A's relative conceptual roles, that is, the set of conceptual roles relative to c for each state c in which A can occur. According to CRS, the content of A is, or is determined by, its conceptual role.

You can get an intuitive feel for this definition by thinking about the consequences in a system Σ of the occurrence of an attitude A. A, of course, has no consequences by itself, but only in the context of a complete state of Σ. So think of completing A somehow, by adding other attitudes and whatever else it takes to make a complete state of Σ. All the paths in Σ's state space that intersect at this state are then all the ways the system can develop from A in the context of that completion, together with all the histories that could lead to A in that completion. A's total conceptual role is just the collection of all its roles relative to some particular completion.[6]

Can we now parlay this account of attitude content into an account of representational content? An attitude has definite effects only in the

5. I am not quite following Schiffer here, of course, for Schiffer supposes that to get belief that I am rich you put a representation with the content that I am rich in the belief box, rather than putting an application with that content in the belief box. See chapter 2 for a discussion of the distinction between applications and representations.

6. Note that CRS cannot distinguish the contents of attitudes that always co-occur in Σ. Note also that we cannot just take the union of the relative conceptual roles, for then we will be unable to distinguish two attitudes whose relative conceptual roles are the same because for every completion of one there is a different completion of the other that yields the same path.

context of a complete cognitive state. A representation has effects by participating in an attitude, that is, by being applied to a target and put in a box (given a semantic and cognitive role). A representation must inherit its epistemic liaisons from the attitudes it makes possible, so, having already defined the conceptual role of an attitude, we can identify the conceptual role of a representation with the set of attitudes it enables. Alternatively, we can proceed as before: Let c be some state containing r. The conceptual role of r relative to c will be the set of paths intersecting at c, and the conceptual role of r will be the set of r's relative conceptual roles.

These definitions allow us to capture precisely the contribution a given representation makes to a cognitive system. Its meaning is identified with the paths through Σ's cognitive space that are made possible by the availability of that representation in the system.[7] Notice, however, that the set of epistemic liaisons determined by a given representation is completely insensitive to which beliefs (or other attitudes) a system *actually* has. It thus does not have the consequence that a failure to share beliefs entails a failure to share meanings.

Why is it generally supposed that CRS inevitably makes what one means depend on what one believes? It arises as follows. One begins with the claim that meaning depends on inferential connections. What one can infer from P, however, depends on what else one believes, unless we count only the strictly analytic consequences of P by itself. We can't do that, however, because there is no analytic/synthetic distinction.[8] So, what is inferable from P depends on what else one believes. So, if meaning depends on inferential connections, what P means depends on what else one believes.

This perspective—the perspective of Σ's current epistemic situation—is appropriate to epistemology, but it isn't appropriate to semantics unless one is a radical verificationist. What I can now infer from P, given what I now believe, might be thought to determine P's epistemic significance for me now. But P's meaning is more plausibly identified with what I could infer from it given a variety of different cognitive contexts. In general, functional roles are always defined in a way that is independent of the state the system happens to be in, for the idea is to capture all the possible connections between states, that is, all the possible paths through state space, not just the one the system happens to be on. This, in fact, makes it

---

7. To get an intuitive handle on what is going on here, it is useful to ask what *net difference* having a given representation r in R_Σ makes to what Σ can do, the difference it makes to the possible transitions between cognitive states. By removing r from R_Σ we remove all the paths through Σ's cognitive state space that involve r-attitudes.

8. Perhaps we can count the logical consequences of P, but these will be of no interest when P is atomic.

clear that the verificationist version of CRS isn't a version of functionalism at all: functional roles are never sensitive to the states a system happens to be in. When you write down a machine table, you have fixed all the functional roles, but you have not said anything about what state the machine is in. A functionalist version of CRS, as opposed to a verificationist version, is not vulnerable even in principle to meaning incomparability objections based on the fact that two systems, or one system at different times, typically does not have all the same attitudes.

Whether verificationist or functionalist, a coherent CRS must come to grips with the fact that it is attitudes, not representations, that have epistemic liaisons, and that epistemic liaisons can only determine representational content indirectly via the attitudes they enable.

CRS, Holism, and the Analytic/Synthetic Distinction

By a *holistic* scheme of representation, I mean a scheme in which the meaning of each representation in the scheme is dependent on the meanings of all the others. It is diagnostic of holistic schemes that adding to or subtracting from the expressive power of the scheme changes the meanings of all the representations in the scheme.[9]

If meaning is what CRS says it is, then schemes of mental representation are typically holistic: adding a new primitive evidently adds to the possible attitudes. It is plausible to assume that these new attitudes will be accessible to or from many of the old states. Evidently, every representation involved in a state that is accessible to or from the new attitude will have a new meaning.[10] Since representational schemes are holistic if CRS is true, and since CRS does not entail meaning-incomparability, it follows that holistic schemes need not involve meaning incomparability. The received view is that CRS can avoid *radical incomparability*, that is, having meaning incomparability follow from a difference in actual attitudes, only by invoking an analytic/synthetic distinction. The idea is to let only the analytic connections count toward the epistemic liaisons that determine meaning, thus insulating meaning from mere differences in "collateral information," though not, of course, from differences in analyticity-conferring

9. This definition differs from those of Fodor and Lepore (1992). Their approach is to say what it is for a *property* to be holistic, viz. that if one thing has it, then lots of things do, and then to focus on whether being meaningful, or having the content *c* is a holistic property. I think this approach is misleading at best. More detailed discussion of atomism and holism can be found in chapter 6. Toward the end of that chapter, I argue that since some schemes of representation are atomistic and some are holistic, meaning itself can be neither.

10. The accessibility assumption is pretty weak: a primitive representation involved in attitudes not accessible to or from any of the old states would be a pretty useless primitive: all the states involving it would be isolated from the rest of the system.

rules of inference. But we now have on the table a respectable formulation of CRS that makes meaning holistic but does not entail radical incomparability, but only a kind of moderate incomparability: systems that share a functional architecture[11] will share meanings. So what goes? Is the received view about the relation between CRS and the analytic/synthetic distinction *wrong*? Or have we smuggled an analytic/synthetic distinction into the formulation of CRS?

Doubtless the main reason for thinking that CRS requires an analytic/synthetic distinction to avoid meaning-incomparability is simply that people have in mind the verificationist version of CRS, not the functionalist version just described. The verificationist version of CRS *does* require the analytic/synthetic distinction to block meaning-incomparability, because the verificationist version does make meaning at t depend on what attitudes Σ has at t. But it is interesting to inquire whether some form of the analytic/synthetic distinction has been smuggled into the functionalist version of CRS as well.

I think it has. CRS does rely on a kind of analytic/synthetic distinction. But it is not *the* analytic/synthetic distinction. Moreover, it is an analytic/synthetic distinction that every orthodox computationalist is already committed to.

Where does an analytic/synthetic distinction come into our formulation of CRS? It comes in with the distinction between the cognitive transitions the system *can* make and the ones it actually does make. If s is on a path in state space that includes an earlier state that involves r, then Σ *can* get to s from an r-state. Of course, it may actually never do so. Whether it does will depend on whether Σ ever gets into the relevant r-state, and on whether the environment cooperates in keeping Σ on the path that leads to s. And that, in turn, depends on previous states and on the world. Still, the assumption of accessibility means that there is a possible route from the one attitude to the other, and that possibility is grounded in the fixed functional architecture of Σ. We can think of the fixed functional architecture as determining which inferences are possible in Σ and which are not.[12] The distinction between which inferences you can make given what you believe and which inferences you can make given how you are built is rather like the distinction between what is synthetically inferable and

11. Given the above conventions, we specify a functional architecture when we specify the intenders, the boxes (cognitive functions), the representational scheme (the set of available representations), and the transition function Σ on cognitive states.

12. Paths through cognitive state space are not quite inferences, of course, because they involve some nonrepresentational states, and because not every transition from one set of attitudes to another is an inference. But paths—at least reasonably short ones—through cognitive state space are inference-like; they are what inferences look like when you look at all the boundary conditions as well as the salient stuff.

what is analytically inferable. Given a representational scheme, intenders, and boxes, the processes are rather like rules of inference, dictating which attitude-to-attitude transitions are possible. From this point of view, CRS, in its functionalist guise, is just a way of saying that the fixed rules of inference—the ones that cannot be learned or unlearned because they are part of the architecture—determine meanings. On this showing, it seems fair enough to say that a functionalist formulation of CRS does rely on a kind of analytic/synthetic distinction.

Those, including me, who don't like the analytic/synthetic distinction, are fond of saying that you can't tell rules from premises. The fact that one goes inevitably from 'bachelor' to 'unmarried' could be due to a rule of inference, making the connection analytic, but could just as well be due to a readily available premise to the effect that all bachelors are unmarried, making the connection synthetic. How is one to know? But in the case of a well-specified computational system, one *does* know, for one knows the difference between fixed functional architecture—the processes, intenders, boxes, and representational scheme that define the system—and the attitudes the system happens to have at a given time—which applications happen to be in which boxes. Anyone who wants to distinguish in this way the structure of the mind from its contents is committed to enough of an analytic/synthetic distinction to save CRS in its functionalist form from radical meaning incomparability. Of course, not everyone is committed to a principled distinction between architecture and content, process, and data. Connectionists, for example, are not. I am not sure how many will be willing to embrace connectionism in order to be in a position to defend the standard objection to CRS. Those who do like to keep a clear distinction between what we believe and how we are built will have to find some other way to bash CRS, or they will have to save their criticism for the verificationist version.

The meaning-incomparability objection to CRS, as it is usually formulated, is seriously confused. Meaning incomparability does not follow from a change in attitudes. But it does follow from a change in representational primitives. Adding (or subtracting) a primitive from a system's representational scheme will alter the meaning of almost everything if it makes any difference at all to the system's cognitive capacities.[13] It will follow that, strictly speaking, new primitives cannot be learned by any inferential process, since there will be no coherent way of describing the inference. Holistic representational schemes generate this kind of incomparability by definition, and CRS makes every scheme holistic. But it is not clear how bad this kind of incomparability really is. Fodor, who does not like holism (Fodor and Lepore, 1992), is notoriously on record

---

13. The same goes for adding (or subtracting) a new (elementary) process, intender, or box.

in support of the view that primitives cannot be inferentially learned anyway (Fodor, 1975). It is true that much of our practice in theory and model building in computational psychology assumes an atomistic scheme of representation, in that we regularly add or subtract primitive representations and processes without supposing that everything changes meaning when we do so. But perhaps this is just bad practice. Philosophy, at any rate, cannot simply assume atomism on the grounds that standard practice seems to presuppose it. Philosophy is, I am sometimes told, supposed to earn its keep by being critical of the unexamined presuppositions of standard practice. We are going to have to forget the incomparability objection to CRS and look elsewhere if we are to see what is wrong with use theories of meaning in general, and CRS in particular.

How CRS Makes Content Explanations Trivial

Here is the plot for the rest of this chapter. I argue first that CRS trivializes explanatory appeals to content. I don't really expect advocates of CRS to disagree with this, but I think it is useful to have the consequence explicitly drawn. I then show that CRS cannot accommodate the distinction between target and content, and hence cannot support a robust notion of representational error. At bottom, it is this failure to come to grips with error that unhinges content explanations for CRS. I also show that CRS cannot distinguish between representation and detection, and relate this to the deflationary approach to content implicit in CRS. I conclude by arguing briefly that explanatory appeals to content are not trivial, as CRS implies they are.

In the story rehearsed in chapter 2 featuring the chess system Σ, we seem to suppose that R_{P3} has the consequences it does in part because of what it represents. Yet the consequences of tokening R_{P3} in these circumstances are part of the epistemic liaisons determined by R_{P3}, hence, according to CRS, part of the specification of R_{P3}'s representational content. It follows that CRSers cannot explain

(D) Σ conceded a draw to black,

by appeal to,

(E)   When the position was P1, Σ erroneously believed that the position after M would be P3,

because CRS renders this explanation trivial. To see this, note that what (E) says, according to CRS, is this:

(E1) Σ's applying R_{P3} to the position-after-m in the belief box yields an attitude A with the epistemic liaisons $\Sigma(A)$, that is, the set of epistemic liaisons associated with A in Σ.

Now (E1) simply *entails* that Σ concedes a draw to black, for conceding a draw in this situation is one of the epistemic liaisons definitive of A. So (E1) entails (E2):

(E2)   The occurrence of A in the situation in question has the consequence that Σ concedes a draw to black,

which is evidently empty as an explanation of (D).

This should come as no surprise. According to CRS, talk of an attitude's content is just shorthand for, among other things, talk of the consequences of its occurrence. So, of course, CRS won't allow you to explain the consequences of the occurrence of an attitude by appeal to that attitude's content. CRS thinks about content as we might think about valence. Imagine a theory that tells us what bonds with what in what proportions. We could simply list all the possibilities (assuming they are finite). Or we could do this: assign a positive or negative number to each radical, and state the following rule: any combination that adds up to zero is a compound.[14] Valences are a kind of fiction in this theory (multiply them all by a constant, and the theory remains unchanged): Specifying something's valence is simply a convenient way of specifying its bonding potential without actually having to mention all the other elements and all the proportions explicitly. Given this fact, it follows that you cannot explain why oxygen bonds with hydrogen in the ratio of one to two by appeal to the valences of oxygen and hydrogen.

CRS gives us a valence theory of content. Content, on this view, is really a kind of fiction, for it treats talk of content as just a convenient way of referring to the epistemic liaisons enabled by a representation without having to mention them explicitly (a useful device, since we typically don't know what the relevant epistemic liaisons are). Once we realize this, it is obvious that CRS isn't going to allow us to explain behavior by appeal to content any more than valence theory is going to allow us to explain bonds by appeal to valence. In both cases, what we wind up with is a kind of thinly disguised joke à la mode de Molière rather than a genuine explanation. CRS trivializes content explanations.[15]

14. This won't actually work, but it might have. Pretend it does work for the sake of the analogy.
15. Block (1986, pp. 668–669) offers two reasons for thinking that CRS doesn't trivialize content explanations: (1) We are talking about a complex disposition that relates the attitude in question to a host of other consequences (and antecedents) besides conceding a draw to black; (2) what Armstrong (1968) called the categorical basis of the disposition can be identified independently of the consequence in question. Neither is persuasive.
    1. You can't explain why opium puts people to sleep by appeal to its dormitival virtue. This situation is not mitigated by noticing that opium also makes people high. If making the disposition complex really changed things, valences would explain bonds!

A lot of you won't be bothered by this, because a lot of you think content is *causally inert* anyway. According to you, content explanations never were in the cards, so their being undermined by CRS is a virtue of CRS, not a vice.

A natural first response to content inertness is this: You can't sustain the position that content is inert when you leave the abstracted heights of philosophy and look at what is actually happening. When I tell you that LOOK-AHEAD comes up with R_{P3}—when I actually show you R_{P3}—you can see that we have got a case of error here, because you can see that R_{P3} represents P3, whereas it ought to represent the position after M, viz. P2. I've set this up for you so that it is easy to see. You can't miss it. And, of course, there's no getting around the fact that it is this error, that is, this misrepresentation of P2 as P3, that causes the trouble.

Though I am sympathetic with this line of response to content inertness, I don't think defenders of CRS need be terribly impressed. They can reply as follows:

We can see what R_{P3} represents *to us*; but we cannot see what R_{P3} represents *to* Σ. For all we know, just looking at R_{P3}, it *does* represent P2 to Σ. The only thing that tells us that we and Σ understand the same thing by R_{P3} is that Σ does such things as mistakenly concede a draw to black in the situation we've been discussing. That is, the only thing that gives us a line on what R_{P3} represents to Σ is the set of epistemic liaisons R_{P3} determines in Σ, and that is just what CRS predicts. The idea that content specifications do more than simply sum up epistemic liaisons as valence specifications sum up chemical liaisons is just an illusion, an illusion created by the fact that the representations in our example have meanings to us that are independent of the epistemic liaisons those representations enjoy in Σ.

Given the availability of this reply, I don't think a brute appeal to the intuition that content explains behavior is going to move the confirmed advocate of CRS to skepticism about the content inertness CRS entails. We have to do better.

I don't want to argue about the causal status of content. But I do want to argue for its explanatory relevance.[16] If CRS is right, there is no point

---

2. Arguing that the categorical basis of a dispositional property explains the disposition's manifestations amounts to conceding that it is not the dispositional property that explains manifestations. You cannot wriggle out of this by identifying a dispositional property with its categorical basis when, as in the case at hand, the disposition in question can be multiply realized—that is, has different categorical bases in different systems or in the same system at different times.

16. All explanation is not causal explanation. See Cummins (1983) for a sustained attempt to show this.

beyond descriptive convenience in the semantic interpretation of the states of a cognitive system. A genuine representationalist, on the other hand, thinks that the status of certain states as representations is of real theoretical importance. If we can show that representationalists are right about this, that is, show that representational content, and hence attitude content, has a genuine explanatory role, then we will have refuted CRS.

CRS and Representational Error

We have shown that CRS trivializes content explanations, but we have yet to determine whether this is a virtue or a vice. My approach to this issue is a bit indirect. Before we get to the explanatory relevance of content, I want to have a look at how CRS deals with error and the distinction between representation and detection. It is the notion of representational error—or, rather, the distinction between error and correctness—that gives content explanation its bite. Intuitively, as I said recently, it is the fact that R_{P3} does not represent what it is supposed to that explains Σ's flawed performance in our running chess system example. I'm going to try to make this intuition do some work by arguing that CRS cannot support a robust conception of error. The basic idea is that CRS will always force you to redescribe an alleged case of error as a case of misinterpretation: any evidence of representational error is better evidence for a different assignment of contents.

The idea that Σ made an error and the idea that Σ is a chess system are based on the same thing, viz. a certain interpretation of Σ's representations, targets, and boxes. But we cannot take that interpretation for granted if, as my imagined CRSer lately claimed, epistemic liaisons provide the only line on what these things mean *in* Σ. Perhaps we should say that Σ is a schess system, and that what it did is a winning move in schess, not a losing move in chess.

Must CRSers take this seriously? I think they must, but it isn't obvious. It isn't obvious because, as remarked earlier, CRS assigns a content to an attitude by assigning a set of epistemic liaisons to it, and this leaves us with no specification of how that content should be expressed. A fully articulated CRS "interpretation" of Σ would leave us entirely in the dark as to whether R_{P3} represents P3, because it would leave us totally in the dark as to whether the attitude that occurred when Σ tokened R_{P3} on the occasion in question had the content *that the position after M is P3*. We can put this point by saying that CRS assigns content determinations to attitudes without actually interpreting them. And in the absence of any interpretations, who is to say whether Σ plays chess or schess, or whether the attitude of interest involved representational error or not?

Surprisingly, we can answer this last question: *There cannot be any error according to CRS.* Think of all the epistemic liaisons determined by R_{P3}: They determine the "use" of R_{P3} in Σ, that is, they determine what targets R_{P3} will be applied to by Σ. Now there must be some factor that fixes interpretation that is independent of use, otherwise there is no sense in asking whether Σ uses R_{P3} erroneously or correctly. We must, in short, have the distinction between what Σ uses r to represent on a given occasion (target), and what r actually represents (content) if we are to make sense of the idea that Σ can misuse r. We have to have a distinction between representational content and target to have error. CRS defines the content of R_{P3} in Σ as its use by Σ, so there can be no question as to whether Σ uses R_{P3} erroneously or correctly.[17] Since, according to CRS, the actual use of R_{P3} in Σ defines the content of R_{P3} in Σ, Σ must use R_{P3} correctly.

So far as I can see, there are only two ways to try to get around this problem: Idealization, and Relativization. Let's look at each in turn.

Idealization
A CRSer might try to allow for error by supposing that content is fixed by ideal use rather than actual use. The trouble with this idea is that it is circular. You cannot understand ideal use as correct use because, in the absence of some criterion of error, you don't know what to idealize away *from*. Σ may be an ideal schess player as it stands. Nor can you identify ideal use with use leading to success or ideal performance. You don't know whether you have success until you know whether you have a chess system or a schess system, and you don't know *that* until you have fixed an interpretation. Put another way, you cannot rule that the bad inferences don't count toward content determination because you don't know what the bad inferences are until you have fixed an interpretation.[18]

A number of moves have been made in response to this difficulty.

Ideal Use Is Rational Use   A number of writers (Dennett, 1987; Davidson, 1973; Pollock, 1989) have tried to salvage the idea that correct use is ideal use by arguing that ideal use can be independently identified as the use required by rationality. The argument goes this way: Intentional explanation presupposes rationality. Since failures of rationality undermine

---

17. Loui (1991) makes a related point when he argues from what amounts to an implicit assumption of CRS to the conclusion that a system that infers '$(x)Gx$' from 'Ga' and the absence of known counterinstances isn't engaged in ampliative inference. The argument is that, in such a system, writing '$Ga \ \& \ -(Ex)$ (it is known that $-Gx$)' is just another way of writing '$(x)Gx$'.

18. You do not want to identify correct inferences with those leading to success in any case, because, as we shall see shortly, misrepresentations and incorrect inferences may, in certain circumstances, be more "successful" than correct ones.

intentional explanation, interpretation is pointless in the absence of rationality. Rationality therefore constrains interpretation. We don't have to worry that we have a perfect "schreasoner" on our hands rather than in imperfect reasoner, because schreasoners do not have intentional states at all. So long, then, as we cleave to intentional explanation, we can take failures of rationality as clues to representational errors.

There are three problems with this line of thought. The first is that rationality cannot be specified in a way that is independent of the facts about how a cognitive system actually works, including the facts about its representational capacities. Rationality cannot, for example:

- Require beliefs that are impossible given a system's representational capacities
- Require beliefs that would take too many resources to acquire or justify
- Require beliefs that would be computationally intractable to use

But if what is rational cannot be abstracted from what is psychologically possible, then rationality cannot provide an independently fixed point that can be used to leverage interpretations. What is rational for a system depends on that system's cognitive architecture, and that, in turn depends on its representational capacities. The proposal under consideration requires, impossibly, a conception of rationality that is logically prior to what a system can or does represent.

The second problem with the idea that representational errors can be identified via deviations from ideal rationality is that content explanations are not, in point of fact, limited to, or even primarily aimed at, the sorts of things that are appropriately assessed for rationality. Indeed, as Fodor has emphasized in another connection (1983), representational explanation has been most successful in the case of processing modules of the sort generally supposed to be involved in early vision and in language processing. These modules are precisely not general-purpose reasoners, and are certainly not straightforwardly subject to epistemological assessments of the sort that are supposed to anchor interpretation.

The third problem with the idea that representational errors can be identified via deviations from ideal rationality is that the explanatory interest of representation is undermined if you define it in terms of rationality. Representationalists want to explain the capacity for cognition generally, and for rationality in particular, by appeal to a prior capacity for representation. This move is undermined if representation is in turn explained in terms of rationality. This, as we noted earlier, doesn't worry the CRSer, because CRSers are antecedently convinced of the explanatory idleness of representation. But it is important to see that the trivialization of representational explanation and the CRSers' typical treatment of error go hand in hand. CRSers aren't trying for a *serious* treatment of error, because they aren't trying for a *serious* treatment of representational explanation in the first place. They are only trying to avoid the embarrassment of having to admit that there isn't any such thing as representational error. But, as Perlman points out (1993), they might as well admit it: the only reason to take representational error seriously is because you take representational explanation seriously. If you don't do the latter, you needn't bother with the former.

Competence and Performance   Distinguishing ideal from actual use is familiar in linguistics as the distinction between competence and performance emphasized by Chomsky (1959). The idea, popularized by Fodor (1975), that mental representations are expressions in a language of thought, encourages a similar distinction between competence and performance in the use of mental representations. It is instructive, therefore, to see why a competence/performance distinction is unavailable to the theory of mental representation.

Linguistic competence is simply ideal linguistic performance, that is, the performance that the system would exhibit but for resource limitations, physical breakdown, and interference from other processes. In computational terms, the underlying assumption is that we are dealing with a system that implements a perfectly general and correct algorithm for language use, but which has limited resources and is dependent on the reliability of its physical instantiation. We might conceive of ideal use of mental representations, then, as the use that would occur but for physical breakdown or resource limitations (assuming these can be identified independently of content assignments). But this is of no help in the present context unless error can be identified with departure from ideal use in this special sense. It is clear, however, that representational error is not always, or even typically, due to breakdown or limited resources. It is much more commonly due to the execution of perfectly good inferential routines that happen to come up with the wrong result because of incomplete or misleading information. These are the uses that are justified but incorrect. If you insist that every use that is unaffected by resource limitations and breakdown is correct, you will be unable to even articulate the distinction between justified use and correct use. You will, in short, become a verificationist. Whatever one thinks of verificationism generally, one doesn't want to be a verificationist about mental meaning, for one wants to be able to take seriously the possibility that cognitive systems are not optimally designed, let alone endowed with a design that is foolproof but for resource limitations and breakdown. CRS will force us to see an ill-designed chess system as a well-designed schess system.

Correct Use Is Adaptive Use   A variation on idealization is to adapt an idea of Millikan's (1984) and construe error as the gap between actual use and Normal use, where Normal use is understood as whatever use was historically crucial in securing the replication of the mechanisms that produce or consume the representations in question, or do both. Correct use, on this conception is, as it were, adaptive use. This approach is attractive because it suggests that a system uses a representation correctly when it uses it in whatever way it *needs* to use it to succeed in the game of life. It seems plausible to suppose that it was those occasions on which representations of edges were applied to edges that made edge representations useful. Hence, it seems plausible to suppose that *r* represents edges just in case its useful applications were to edges.

Note the two-step strategy here. First, representational content is defined in terms of *correctness*, the idea being to identify *r*'s content with its target on occasions of correct use: *r* represents edges just in case it is correct when its target is an edge. Second, correctness is defined in terms of adaptation: correct uses are adaptive uses. This reverses the strategy I have been pursuing, which defines correctness in terms of content and target, and hopes for independent definitions of these. Either way, however, error turns out to be a mismatch between target and content, and both strategies require an independent treatment of target fixation.

There is no objecting to the truth of step 1: it is tautological that *r* represents edges iff it is correctly applied to edges. The issue is rather one of explanatory strategy, since step 1 is of no use unless one can define correctness independently of content. The burden thus falls squarely on step 2, the step that explains correctness as adaptive use. There are three reasons why I don't think this will work.

1. *Adaptiveness does not correspond to correctness.* There are two sides to this: A representation can be correct but not be adaptive, and it can be adaptive without being correct. (a) *Correct but not adaptive.* You can design a trout that, in spite of refraction, correctly represents the positions of insects flying just above the water, but this will not be adaptive in a trout already equipped with a jumping routine that compensates for refraction. (b) *Adaptive but not correct.* These are the cases in which the errors are not *serious.* A system that consistently represents little ambient black particles as insects will serve a trout well in an environment in which enough of the little ambient black particles are insects, and few are harmful. It is cheaper to design a tolerant digestive system in such circumstances than it is to design an insect recognition system free of false positives. Efficiency often entails inaccuracies in a resource-bounded system. In such systems, inaccuracies that are efficient but not serious will be more adaptive than more accurate but less efficient alternatives.

2. *Adaptational stories cannot distinguish correlated contents.* This is the point Fodor makes against teleological theories (Fodor, 1990b). If being F and being G are correlated in an organism's environment, the adaptiveness of representing F and of representing G will be the same (provided the computational costs are comparable). Fodor points out that evolutionary theory won't distinguish between a story in which a representation r in a frog's visual system represents flies and one in which it represents ambient particles provided that r triggers the snapping mechanism, and provided that there is enough of a correlation between ambient particles and flies. The correlation need not even be lawlike; it can be pure coincidence. Coincidences will get selection jobs done just as well as laws, provided they last long enough, as every operant conditioning experiment shows.

3. *Adaptational stories get the explanatory order wrong.* Representations, when they are adaptive, are adaptive because they represent what they do. Think of cognitive maps (Tolman, 1948): They are adaptive because they are isomorphic to the spaces they map; they are not isomorphic to the spaces they map because they are adaptive.[19] Explaining correctness in terms of adaptation gets matters backward. The adaptational theory is motivated by the fact that it is plausible (though not quite right; see [1]) to suppose that correct uses of a representation are adaptive. But what makes this plausible is the idea that the uses in question are adaptive because they are correct. That motivation is undermined on the assumption that the uses in question are correct because they are adaptive. To a first approximation, representationalists want to explain cognitive success in terms of representational correctness. But you cannot do *that* if you explain representational correctness in terms of the adaptiveness of cognitive success.

The idea that the correct use of a mental representation is its ideal or Normal use is a dead end, then. The alternative is to relativize. If you can't find a principled distinction between saying a system is playing chess and making representational errors and saying it is playing schess and getting everything right, then make a virtue of necessity: say it is both. It is chess relative to one interpretation (I_c) and schess relative to another (I_s).[20] When Σ applies R_{P3} to the position-after-m, it makes an error relative to I_c, but not relative to I_s. This allows for error at the price of abandoning CRS altogether. For this suggestion amounts to saying that, if we fix con-

19. You cannot get around this by arguing that what makes the isomorphism representational is the fact that it has a selection history. Since it is the isomorphism itself that does all the explanatory work, insisting that it isn't a *representation* of the space it maps until it has a selection history just prices you out of the market, for it makes the property of being a representation explanatorially irrelevant. For an extended treatment of this theme, see chapter 7.
20. This, I blush to admit, was the route I took in *Meaning and Mental Representation*.

tent assignments in advance somehow, then we can tell error from correctness, and hence can tell success from failure. While this is true enough, it is clear that epistemic liaisons are no longer playing a role in determining content.

The Nontriviality of Representational Explanation

CRS offers us a valence theory of meaning which more or less self-consciously trivializes representational explanation. This, of course, is an embarrassment to CRS only if representational explanation is not trivial.

The difficulty is not, of course, that CRS gets the causal properties of representation wrong. Indeed, CRS gets them right by definition since it, in effect, identifies r's content with its relevant causal properties. As long, then, as we think that what we are after is an accurate picture of the causal structure, it will be impossible to see how CRS could possibly miss something of explanatory importance.[21] It follows from this observation that the explanatory role of content is not to be found in its causal role. To see where it is found, you have to appreciate that it is the notion of representational error that gives representational explanation its bite. Representational error, as we have seen, depends on a distinction between how a representation is used, and what it means. Since use theories explicitly deny this distinction, they undermine the notion of representational error and with it the explanatory importance of representation.

As we saw in chapter 3, it is the distinction between representational correctness and error, or, better, between representational accuracy and inaccuracy, that allows one to exploit the distinction between the degree of inaccuracy and its seriousness, and correlatively between effective representation and accurate representation. And it is what allows one to exploit the distinction between forced and unforced error, and between forced error and the inability to exploit an adequate representation or scheme. Let's look briefly at what this is going to cost.

Effectiveness vs. Accuracy

As we saw in chapter 3, less accurate representations can sometimes be more effective than more accurate alternatives because of the computational costs in achieving accuracy in the first place, and in manipulating highly accurate representations once they are achieved. Accurate predator recognition is bound to be slow, and, given the relatively insignificant

---

21. This, I think, is the key to understanding Stich's syntactic theory of mind (1983). If you are an orthodox computationalist, then you think that the causal properties of representations turn on their syntax. From this, and the assumption that it is causal structure we are after, it simply follows that content is irrelevant.

consequences of false positives, a faster system that generates many false positives is likely preferable. Without a distinction between a representation's use and its meaning, you cannot coherently articulate this simple observation. Any reason to suspect false positives will be a better reason to suspect misinterpretation, for applying a representation to a passing cloud or the shadow it makes will count as a misuse only against some independent standard of what the representation means and hence of how it should be used. In this context, it is easy to see why adaptationist standards of correct use cannot be right. For the use of r that accounts for the replication of its producers/consumers need not be the right use on any particular occasion. Indeed, given the efficiency of a policy that tolerates false positives, applications to nonpredators surely were among the uses that contributed critically to the replication of the users and consumers of that representation. *The point about the efficiency of a policy that tolerates false positives is that it is adaptive.* It follows that appeals to adaptiveness cannot distinguish correct uses from incorrect uses. Use theories undermine the important distinction between accuracy and effectiveness because that distinction requires a notion of representational content that is independent of use.

Forced and Unforced Error
We arrive at a similar conclusion when we reflect on the distinction between forced and unforced error. To take an example familiar from the history of philosophy, the Kantian position that the human visual system constructs Euclidean images makes the introspectively plausible prediction that we will be unable to imagine or see non-Euclidean spaces accurately. The Kantian position treats the visual representation of non-Euclidean space as a case of forced (but not serious) error.[22] If we adopt a use theory of meaning, however, we will be unable to articulate this position and the issues it raises, for we will have to suppose that visual representations, since they are never[23] applied to non-Euclidean space, are themselves non-Euclidean in content! Use theories cannot contemplate the possibility of forced error because that requires representations that never correctly apply.

In just the same way, use theories will be unable to construe the dispute between Piagetians and their opponents concerning the shifting patterns of mistakes developmental psychologists observe in the performance of children on word arithmetic problems, for that dispute just is a dispute about whether the mistakes are due to forced representational error or to

22. Kant, of course, didn't think Euclidean representation of space was erroneous, but we do.
23. Or almost never—certainly never in detection cases (causal theories) or cases with selective significance (adaptationist theories).

developmentally significant changes in the capacity to exploit adequate innate representational sources (see D. Cummins, 1988, 1991). Use theories are bound to see this as a pseudo-issue founded on misinterpretation. Since they are bound to collapse the distinction between forced error and the inability to exploit existing representational resources, they will see the relevant development as either a case of meaning change (verificationist version) or as a kind of frequency effect in which the frequency of certain uses drops and the frequency of others rises as a function of cognitive changes (functionalist version). The hypothesis, shared by most parties to the dispute in the developmental literature, that systematic mistakes are due to systematic misrepresentation, is simply not available to use theories.[24]

The Moral of the Story
Suppose I'm right: cognitive science requires a robust notion of representational error, and use theories cannot provide one. *Why* do we need the notion of representational error? It is one thing to see that certain scientific issues presuppose the notion of representational error, as we've just done. That shows *that* we need misrepresentation, but not *why*. It is quite another thing to have a philosophical account of the role of representation in explanation that allows us to see why a scientific understanding of cognition requires a serious conception of content, one that makes misrepresentation possible by keeping meaning and use apart.

To see what representationalism really buys you, you need a theory of representation. I'm going to try to provide one in chapter 7. But even without a theory of representation in hand, you can see enough to keep you moving in the right direction. Appeals to representation buy two different things.

Dimension Shifts   Semantic interpretation effects a dimension shift that reveals mere computation as something epistemically assessable: the manipulation of formally individuated objects is revealed as addition, or planning, or language processing. Since cognitive capacities are capacities for epistemic constraint satisfaction, and since epistemic constraints are defined semantically, that is, defined over semantically individuated objects, explaining cognition by appeal to computation requires semantically interpreting the objects computed.

This much is available to the advocate of CRS. This is the account of the explanatory role of content I offered in *Meaning and Mental Representation* in connection with the functional role theory of content offered

---

24. Carey (1985) clearly endorses some form of CRS, yet helps herself to the notion of representational error. As she must: developmental psychology without representational error is hopeless.

there (Cummins, 1989). If the sort of dimension shift just described is all one sees of the explanatory role of representation, then CRS can seem a very plausible story. Imagine a device, m, that looks like a calculator. When m is given '19', '18' and '25' as inputs, m generates a '2' in the rightmost position of the output buffer. At this point, m's target is the current carry, 20. Device m constructs '10', and generates a '5' in the next output position. Given these facts, we could say the thing is an adder that has misrepresented a carry, or we could say that it is a shmadder (like an adder except . . .). There appears to be little to choose between these stories. There is no *substantive* dispute here about what m does, and we can explain the performance of an embedding system in terms of the incorporation of a faulty adder, or in terms of the incorporation of a successful shmadder, for, in both cases, the point is to contrast the performance we actually get with the performance we would get if we incorporated a successful adder.

Reasoning vs. Representation   As long as we focus on cases like this in which semantic interpretation enters only to bridge the gap between, say, a description in terms of symbols and one in terms of numbers, the notion of representational error plays no significant role, and so use theories seem perfectly adequate. What, then, does the notion of misrepresentation buy us? Or equivalently, what do we gain from a clear distinction between what a representation means (content) and how it is used (target)?

A use-independent notion of content or accuracy allows one to distinguish the correctness of a representation from the correctness of reasoning (or other processing) done with it. If we misrepresent the facts to Holmes, he will misidentify the culprit, even though he reasons flawlessly. Similarly, distorted memories about parents may mislead an excellent planner, resulting in botched plans for a wedding. CRS, however, must see this as inadequate *planning*. If we follow CRS in this, however, we will have a hard time explaining why plans that don't involve taking into account the personal characteristics of family members work fine. Distinguishing meaning and use allows us to factor cognition into representation problems and reasoning problems. The flexibility that results from allowing for the interaction of these independent factors is what gives representationalist accounts of cognition the descriptive and explanatory power needed to understand the value of fast but error-prone predator recognition systems, or to understand how to reconcile developmental stages in the ability to solve word arithmetic problems with the impressive evidence for the innateness of arithmetical concepts (Wynn, 1992).

Conclusion

The standard objection to CRS is off target. CRS does not, when given a functionalist rather than a verificationist formulation, have the consequence that systems with different beliefs are meaning-incomparable. The consequence of radical meaning-incomparability is blocked by the mediation of a kind of analytic/synthetic distinction, but it is a kind of analytic/synthetic distinction that every orthodox computationalist must accept, for it is just the distinction between what Σ can do given its architecture, and what it can do given its current attitudes. CRS *does* have the consequence that meaning is holistic—that systems with different primitives are incomparable—but it isn't clear whether that is a bad consequence. It would mean that we could not describe acquisition of a new primitive as inferential learning, but Fodor (1975) has argued persuasively for that on independent grounds anyway.

CRS is wrong, but not because it engenders radical meaning-incomparability. It is wrong because it trivializes content explanation. It trivializes content explanation because, like all use theories of meaning, it cannot support a robust notion of representational error, and its explanatory potential is thereby deprived of a crucial degree of freedom. Use theories have trouble with representational error because the concept of representational error, and hence of the misuse of a representation, requires a distinction between how a representation is used and what it means. Use theories all have a two-step structure: They identify r's content with its target in cases of correct use, and then they attempt to specify some naturalistic sufficient condition of correct use. It is the second step that causes the trouble, and it is not hard to see why. Under what condition is the use of a representation guaranteed to be correct? The history of epistemology should teach us that nothing *guarantees* accuracy. Or rather: The only conditions that guarantee accuracy also trivialize content. For example: You can make believing a sense datum statement a sufficient condition for its truth, but the price you pay is that you empty it of evidential value. If s is evidence of something else, t, then any evidence against t is, indirectly, evidence against s. If s is to be immune in principle to counterevidence, it cannot be evidence for anything else. Epistemological conditions of correct use (e.g., r is correctly applied to t by Σ if Σ knows that t satisfies r) are bound to violate the *Explanatory Constraint* laid down in chapter 1, since we want representation to explain cognition and not the other way around. Nonepistemological conditions of correct use are bound to fail, for nature never guarantees accurate representation.

Chapter 5
Causal Theories

Identifying the Target

What I am calling causal theories of content—CTs hereafter—have been all the rage for some time now. They are frequently called informational theories, and I called them covariance theories in *Meaning and Mental Representation* (Cummins, 1989). The most prominent contemporary versions are to be found in Stampe (1977), Fodor (1987), and Dretske (1981), though there are many others, and the idea goes back at least to Locke.[1]

CTs are use theories, and all use theories work the same way: since the content of r is its target on an occasion of correct use, we can fix the content of r if we can identify its target on occasions of correct use. CTs identify targets by focusing on detection: the target of a representation tokened by a detector on occasions when it detects successfully is the property that causes the representation to be tokened. So if you can identify occasions on which a detector succeeds, you know the content of the representation it tokens is the property that causes the representation to be tokened on those occasions.

Suppose, for instance, that a system Σ tokens r in response to the property H of being a horse. Of course, there are lots of perfectly correct ways to respond to H other than by tokening a |horse|. But the causal theorist has in mind a context in which the point is to *detect* a certain property. A property detector in the presence of the property H should token a |horse|. If we can specify some condition under which our detector is bound to succeed, that is, to apply the correct representation, then we know the content of that representation is the property that causes it. This is, as remarked above, an instance of the general strategy behind use theories:

SCHEMA FOR USE THEORIES: (1) Focus on some intender INT; (2) identify some condition C under which INT is bound to succeed, that is, bound to generate a correct representation; (3) identify INT's target in tokening r when C obtains; (4) identify the content of r with INT's target in tokening r when C obtains.

---

1. See Cummins (1989) for the Lockean origins of the theory.

CTs focus on detectors as the intenders of choice (1). They do this be-cause they know how to identify a detector's target: the target of a repre-sentation correctly produced by a detector is the property that caused it, and that takes care of (3).[2] It remains to deal with (2), that is, to find some way of identifying occasions on which detectors apply their representa-tions correctly, and it is here that CTs divide into different flavors.

There are three basic flavors of CT. Epistemological theories (Stampe, 1977; Fodor, 1987) attempt to specify epistemological conditions under which detectors apply their representations correctly. Teleological theo-ries claim that detectors apply their representations correctly when they are functioning properly, and take the main problem to be one of giving a satisfactory account of proper functioning (Millikan, 1984; Papineau, 1987). Fodor's asymmetric dependence theory (Fodor, 1990b) identifies the occasions of successful detection as those that are instances of a spe-cial kind of law, viz. one that is not asymmetrically dependent on any other law governing a detector's use of the same representation. Seeing each of these theories as variations on the basic schema for use theories, and, in particular, seeing them as differing in how they meet requirement (2) of that schema, provides a new and helpful perspective on them. Be-cause all use theories work the same way, they are all subject to the same three difficulties we encountered in connection with CRS:

• First, use theories require, for every representation, naturalistic conditions under which use of that representation is guaranteed to be correct, and these are simply not in the cards.

• Second, use theories give us, in the first instance, the content of a use, that is, of an application, not of a representation, and you can-not identify the content of a representation with the content of any of its applications.

• Finally, use theories have a general problem satisfying the Ex-planatory Constraint because their game is to pin the right contents on the right representations, not to tell us what representing IS. I will take up these problems in turn.

Problem 1: When Are Detectors Foolproof?

Never. That's the problem in a nutshell: there just is no non-question-begging way to specify a condition under which a detector is guaranteed to generate a representation that matches a substantive target.[3]

---

2. CTs thus have the consequence that, for primitives at any rate, you cannot mean what you cannot detect, an empiricist assumption that has a pretty dismal track record.

3. Nonsubstantive targets are easy to hit. For example, a detector whose function it is to de-tect some mathematical truth or other can simply output "1 = 1" all the time. Nothing like this is going to work with targets like predators or protons.

Epistemological Variations

FORM: *r* represents *c* in Σ = *df* a detector in Σ operating under epistemologically optimal or ideal conditions produces *r* in response to *c*.

Theories of this form are inevitably verificationist, for they are in the position of having to specify an epistemological condition under which misrepresentation by a detector is impossible, and this will amount to assimilating satisfaction conditions to evidence conditions. It is just a fact of life that, even under optimal or ideal conditions, detectors can fail. The only way to avoid this fact of life is to embrace some form of antirealism, that is, to *identify* what there is to detect with whatever gets detected under optimal or ideal conditions. But saving a causal theory of representation by becoming an antirealist is perverse: if you are an anti-realist, why would you be attracted to the idea that mental representations mean the distal properties that cause them to be produced by detectors? You do not think there is a mind-independent world to represent anyway. I can imagine someone trying a causal solution to the problem of representation *first*, and then giving the whole thing an antirealist reading *afterward*, in the interest of a general theory of knowledge, say. But bringing in anti-realism to save CT is like killing children to prevent childhood diseases. Antirealism undoes the idea that there are mind-independent distal properties out there causing detectors in the mind to token representations of them.

Teleological Variations

FORM: *r* represents *c* in Σ = *df* a properly functioning detector in Σ produces *r* in response to *c*

Teleological variations of CT rely on the idea that properly functioning detectors apply their representations correctly. The basic problem, then, is to formulate a theory of proper functioning that is naturalistic and that has the desired consequence that properly functioning detectors detect correctly.

It is important to distinguish two senses of proper functioning in this connection. In one sense, a detector is functioning properly when it is playing its psychological role the way it is supposed to. In another sense, a detector is functioning properly when it is playing its semantic role the way it is supposed to, that is, when it is detecting correctly. The distinction is important because it is possible for a detector to function properly psychologically while not functioning properly semantically. Limited resources may dictate that optimal psychological functioning will inevitably involve a good deal of representational error. Predator recognition systems that are fast enough to be of any use will generate a great many false positives. The fact that psychological and semantic functioning can and do come apart creates an insuperable problem for teleological versions of CT, for the basic tactic of the teleological approach is to define correct semantic functioning in terms of good psychological functioning. The problem can be illustrated by considering Millikan's version of the theory which holds that the proper function of d in Σ is to detect c iff d was replicated because it produced representations of c (Millikan, 1984). As we saw in chapter 4, it is a mistake to identify the adaptive uses of a representation with its correct uses. One is entitled to assume that adaptive uses are those that contribute to psychological success,[4] but not that adaptive uses are those that contribute to semantic success. Misrepresentations can and do contribute to psychological success in systematic and important ways, and can therefore be adaptive. In systems with limited resources, inaccuracies that are efficient but not serious will be more adaptive than more accurate but less efficient alternatives.[5]

This problem is bound to arise for any teleological theory: proper psychological functioning just does not guarantee correct semantic functioning. The premise that an intender having c as its target tokens r when it is functioning properly will not give us the conclusion that r means c unless we can assume that properly functioning intenders represent correctly. We cannot assume this if we have psychological functioning in mind. But if we have semantic functioning in mind, then the account is trivially circular, for then the premise in question reduces to the claim that an intender that has c as its target tokens r when it represents c correctly. Teleological theories are constitutionally incapable of saying anything about the conditions under which the use of a representation is correct without falling into one of these two traps.

For another concrete illustration, consider Dretske's account (1981): r means $C = df$ the function of r is to indicate C. As it stands, this is hopeless because representations have lots of functions other than indicating something. It is not the function of "beer" to indicate beer in "If the beer

---

4. Adaptive uses are really those that contribute to biological success, but this won't affect the argument at all.

5. I don't want to give the impression that Millikan's theory is necessarily a version of CT, though she usually presents it that way. Her theory can be given a much more general form: r represents c in $\Sigma = df$ the proper function of IN (some intender or other) is to represent c, and IN was replicated because of the occasions on which it tokened r. The idea is that c is IN's target, and IN's uses of r are correct because adaptive. Once you have the (false) assumption that adaptive uses of r are correct, all you need is to identify the target of r on the occasion of an adaptive use. As in all use theories, the fact that content = target on occasions of correct use does the rest.

is in the refrigerator, it is cold." But we can see what Dretske has in mind: tokening |beer| in a detector has the function of indicating beer, for a detector is just an intender whose function is to indicate its targets. So we might say that what makes *r* mean beer is that properly functioning indicators token *r* in response to beer. But we shouldn't say it, unless we are convinced that properly functioning indicators always represent correctly. We should be convinced but unimpressed if "proper functioning" in this formula means proper semantic functioning. And we should be unconvinced if "proper functioning" means proper psychological functioning.

It's worth noting that it isn't the teleology *per se* that is the problem here. You could have a theory that says that *r* represents *c* iff the function of *r* (not its uses) is blah-blah.[6] The problem arises when you embed the teleology in a use theory (like CT), for the function of the *use* of a representation is to hit its target, not to represent its content.[7] The TRUE-OF does not reduce to the GOOD-FOR any more than the TRUE reduces to the GOOD.

Asymmetric Dependence (AD)

Fodor has proposed a version of CT that appears to be neither epistemological nor teleological. Fodor's theory is this:

(AD) *r* represents *P* (i.e., is satisfied by things having *P*) in Σ if:

1. Sometimes, something having *P* actually causes *r* to be tokened in Σ.
2. It is a law in situ that something's having *P* causes *r* to be tokened in Σ.
3. All cases in which *r* is tokened in Σ that are not caused by something's having *P* are asymmetrically dependent on the law mentioned in (2).

To see how this is supposed to work, remember our friend Rover who has been conditioned to respond to the sound of a bell in the same way he responds to food. We can diagram the situation as in figure 5.1. After conditioning, hearing the bell causes a |BELL| in Rover's CURRENT-STIMULUS-intender. Because conditioning has left a |BELL ⊃ FOOD| in memory, however, Rover now puts a |FOOD| in his EXPECTED-STIMULUS-intender, which leads him to salivate. Given this setup,

---

6. Of course, you cannot really have a theory like this. My point is just that the problem I've been discussing doesn't arise out of the teleology itself, but out of the interaction between teleology and CT when the former is recruited to solve the problem use theories have about specifying conditions of correct use.

7. Teleological stories, we will see later (chapter 8), do nicely as theories of target fixation. Teleological stories can tell us what a representation is supposed to represent on a given occasion of its use, and that, of course, is just the target of that representational episode.

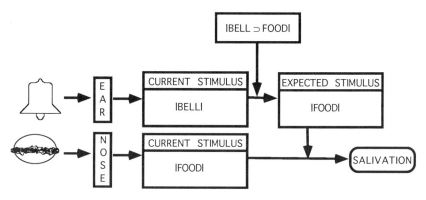

Figure 5.1
Flow diagram of a dog conditioned to salivate to a bell.

1. Sometimes, a bell ringing actually causes |FOOD| to be tokened in Σ.
2. It is a law in situ that a bell's ringing causes |FOOD| to be tokened in Σ.

But, of course, bell sounds are not the target of |FOOD|s applied by the expected-stimulus intender; food is. Clause 3 of AD, the clause that gives it its name, is designed to make room for the ringing bell-to-|FOOD| connection on the grounds that it is asymmetrically dependent on the food-to-|FOOD| connection.[8] The fundamental idea is that property-to-representation connections fix content only when they are basic, that is, not asymmetrically dependent on other such connections.

Notice that AD won't work unless we assume that the basic connections are all cases of detection. For only in detection is a representation caused by its target. If basic connections occur in which P causes r, but P is not r's target, AD will assign P as r's content even though, by hypothesis, this would be a case of error. AD, like any use theory, works by identifying r's content with its target in cases of correct use. What AD tells us, is that r's content is its cause in those cases in which r's production by a detector in Σ is an instance of a basic law in situ. So AD must assume that every instance of a basic law of detection is a case of correct representation. Given that every instance of a basic law is a case of correct detection, it follows that the antecedents of such laws specify the contents of their consequents.

8. Note that this is not a case of error: ringing bells ought to cause |FOOD|s in Rover: that is the point of the conditioning. But these |FOOD|s are not applied to their distal causes (bells); their targets are rather expected stimuli, namely food.

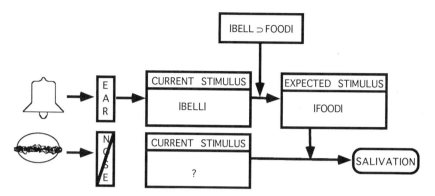

Figure 5.2
Flow diagram of a dog with severed olfactory nerve conditioned to salivate to a bell.

Assessing AD's Enabling Assumptions   AD makes two enabling assumptions that often go unnoticed: the first is that every basic law governs detection; the second is that every instance of a basic law is a case of correct representation. I propose to examine these briefly in turn.

Consider again the case of Rover (shown again in figure 5.2). Suppose that, after conditioning, Rover's olfactory nerve is cut, as indicated. If we assume that all food detection is mediated by smell, it will no longer be a law that food causes |FOOD|s in Rover. What shall we say about the content of *r*? It will, of course, still be a law that ringing bells cause *rs*. But that law cannot be asymmetrically dependent on food detection, since Rover can no longer detect food. According to AD, it seems that *rs* must be |BELL|s. But, besides being wildly counterintuitive, this sorts ill with the fact that Rover still salivates to ringing bells. How will the explanation go if *rs* are |BELL|s? The assumption is that there is an unconditioned connection between |FOOD|s and salivation. Before his surgery, Rover's reasoning mechanisms used a |BELL| and a |BELL ⊃ FOOD| to generate a |FOOD|, which then generated salivation. Since Rover continues to salivate to the bell, it seems we must say either that *rs* are still |FOOD|s, contrary to AD, or that the content of *r* is not a factor, before or after Rover's operation, in his salivation to the bell. If we opt for the latter treatment, we must also abandon the idea, dear to Fodor's heart at least, that conditioning is mediated by establishing a |BELL ⊃ FOOD| in Rover.[9]

9. A determined defender of AD might opt for an emendation which requires, in effect, that the bell-to-|FOOD| connection be asymmetrically dependent on a food-to-|FOOD| connection having held at some previous time. Fodor, however, rightly insists that asymmetrical dependencies be assessed synchronically in order to avoid a different kind of counterexample (see, e.g., Fodor 1987).

The idea that every basic law is a law governing detection is radically implausible. Rover is one kind of counterexample, but there are many more. Consider any case of reasoning that is basic. Suppose, as seems likely, that modus ponens is a feature of the architecture of human reason (Braine, 1978; Rips, 1983). Then it will be a basic law of human psychology that anything of the form $(A \supset B)\&A$ will cause something of the form B. Since the causal connection is governed by form, the cause of B is the occurrence of something of the form $(A \supset B)\&A$, but the property of having the form $(A \supset B)\&A$ need not be the content of B. The content of a conclusion is not the form of the premises that cause it. In general, any feature of the architecture that underwrites a move from one representational state to another will be a basic law. But, of course, these are almost never cases in which the content of the effect state is the property of the representational state that caused it. Fundamental laws of reasoning are just the most obvious cases in point. In the light of this, it seems pretty evident that AD should be revised to require that content-fixing laws be not only basic but govern detection. Revised thus, AD simply stipulates that basic laws not governing detection don't count. CT really cannot escape being about detection, for only detectors are in the business of representing the properties that cause them to generate representations.[10]

The second enabling assumption of AD, that instances of basic laws are cases of correct representation, is really our main concern here, for we are trying to see how CTs deal with the problem of specifying conditions of correct use. AD has to convince us that representational error is never a basic feature of detection architecture.

Assumptions about what is asymmetrically dependent on what are empirical assumptions. The asymmetric dependence of some causal connections on others is what makes legitimate scientific idealization possible. Consider the ideal pendulum law, $T = 2\pi\sqrt{(l/g)}$. This law idealizes away from the effects of friction and air resistance. What makes this idealization legitimate is the fact that the effect of friction and air resistance on period is asymmetrically dependent on the effect of length and gravity. There is such a thing as the period a pendulum would have if there were no friction or air resistance, but there is no such thing as the period it would have if there were there no length or gravity.[11] The relation between period, on the one hand, and length and gravity on the other, is a basic relation, given by the ideal pendulum law. In contrast, there is no general relation between friction and period, or between air resistance and period,

---

10. I'm not sure how CT could define 'detector' naturalistically. I don't think there is much to be learned by pressing this objection, however.
11. We can, of course, make the simplifying (though not idealizing) assumption that gravity is a constant, for there is such a thing as the way the pendulum would behave were gravity constant.

that can be independently stated in the form $T = f$(friction) or $T = g$(air resistance).

With this understanding of asymmetric dependence, we are in a position to see that AD's assumption that detection can be error-free amounts to the assumption that representational error stands to detection as friction stands to the period of a pendulum. According to AD, cases of error in content-fixing detection must be asymmetrically dependent on correct detection, and this amounts, as we've just seen, to the assumption that it is legitimate to idealize away from error in detection. Moreover, since limited resources make error inevitable, AD is committed to the claim that it is legitimate to idealize away from resource constraints in detection. And that claim, I will argue, is false.

It is important to understand what the assumption of the possibility of resource-free detection really means. It means that the *actual* mechanisms underlying detection would operate error-free if they were provided with unlimited resources. But this is surely wrong. Most actual natural detection systems are designed for operation with fixed resources. Adding resources to such architectures would not change their operation at all. For most detectors are designed to work by keying on one or more surface features that are correlated with the target well enough to avoid immediately compromising the survival of the genotype. More resources don't help these systems because, as it were, they have no deep theory to exploit.

A common response to this is to argue such systems don't really detect the alleged target but only the correlated surface features. But Fodor rightly resists this move on the grounds that it undermines the capacity of the theory to account for the representation of anything but surface features and their combinations.

A different response is to argue that the detection of distal properties is backed up by a system that is bound to get the right answer given enough time and memory, namely Reason. It is perfectly true that when I take a cow for a horse, adding more resources is likely to correct my mistake, because, given enough time, I can learn about cows and horses, consult the experts, and so on. But there is no *guarantee* that I will ever get it right. Perhaps this cow looks very much like a horse, and I am a very stubborn person. More important, horse recognition that is mediated by the sorts of processes that would be helped by more resources could not possibly be fool-proof. Resource-intensive horse recognition depends on nondemonstrative inference, and it is a consequence of this obvious fact that cognitive architecture in the horse recognition business can have no fool-proof procedure to fall back on if it is just given enough time and memory to use it. To suppose otherwise is to embrace an antirealism that takes the truth just to be whatever reason converges on in the limit. And we are not talking about "right reason" here, but human reason, designed as evolution patched it together.

Let's summarize. AD requires that basic detection, that is, detection that is an instance of a basic law in situ, must be error-free. Cow-to-|horse| connections must be asymmetrically dependent on horse-to-|horse| connections. Errors must stand to detection as friction stands to the period of a pendulum. But the assumption that basic laws of detection idealize away from error entails that basic laws of detection also idealize away from resource constraints, for resource constraints are bound, in general, to engender error. Witness fast predator detection. But basic laws of detection do not idealize away from resource constraints. Adding more resources wouldn't help a natural detector at all unless it were backed up by Reason. And even that wouldn't make detection fool-proof, for the only kind of reason that can help here is nondemonstrative reason, and the only way to make that fool-proof under idealization is to embrace antirealism. As I pointed out in connection with epistemological versions of CT, no representationalist should save a theory of content by adopting antirealism, for antirealism is the view that there is no mind-independent world to represent. AD is no better at solving the problem of specifying conditions of correct use than the other versions of CT.

Problem 2: CT and the Content/Attitude Distinction

CT faces a problem analogous to the one that plagues CRS, namely that it is sensitive to attitude content, not representational content. This is because CTs fix content in terms of detections, and detections are attitudes, not representations. To detect a horse, it is not enough to token a |horse| in response to a horse; the |horse| must be tokened by the right intender. Consider Rover again. A |food| produced by the CURRENT-STIMULUS intender in response to food counts as detecting food; a |food| produced by the CURRENT-GOAL intender, or by the EXPECTED-STIMULUS intender, in response to food does not count as detecting food. To detect H, then, is to token an attitude whose content is (at least in part) that there is H present in response to H's being present.

As we have seen, however, it is possible for Σ to have an attitude with the content that there is H present, even if Σ cannot represent H at all! Imagine Σ designed with a FOOD-STATUS intender which typically generates such representations as |present| or |absent|. When a |present| is produced by the FOOD-STATUS intender in response to food, Σ constructs an attitude whose content is that food is present, and thereby detects the presence of food. But Σ does not thereby represent food, nor is the fact that it is a law in situ, that is, a law of Σ's nature, that food causes this attitude any reason to think its constituent representation means food. By construction, it does not; it means *present*, the property something has in virtue of being nearby, in the vicinity. Once we see that detections are attitudes, it is obvious how to construct two systems that are capable of exactly the same detections but that are representationally disjoint. It follows from the possibility of such constructions that appealing to the causes of detections cannot pin down representational contents.[12]

Putting a |present| in the FOOD-STATUS-BOX is rather like putting an X in a box on a questionnaire:

Married: yes ☐ no ☐

We can and should distinguish what you mean by putting an X in the yes box from what the X that you put there means. Being able to make an X does not give you the capacity to represent being married, though it does give you, in this context, the capacity to state that you are married. This is why multiple-choice examinations, or true-false examinations, are easier than those that require you to write out your own answers: multiple-choice and true-false examinations require little expressive power on the part of the student. All the attitude's content is in the target specification. One just has to pick an attitude. The representational content of the X is disappearingly small: in this context, it means something like "this one," as is indicated by the fact that one could get the same result simply by pointing to an alternative.

Earlier we saw that CTs generally are instances of the general use theory schema. What does the work in use theories is the fact that content equals target on occasions of correct use. We are now in a position to appreciate even more clearly how this strategy of identifying contents with targets in cases of correct use depends on a precise identification of the targets. Merely knowing that when D tokens r, Σ constructs an attitude with the content that the most common prey of cats is mice, and that this is a case of correct representation, gives us little information about what the content of r might be. We might have a |mouse| tokened by a MOST-COMMON-PREY-OF-CATS intender, or a |cat| tokened by a MICE-ARE-THE-MOST-COMMON-PREY-OF intender, or any of many other alternatives. So when a causal theorist assumes that the target in the case of a horse detection is the property of being a horse, we have an assumption of a kind that is quite generally unwarranted: one cannot infer representational content from attitude content even when one knows there is no error.

---

12. The FOOD-STATUS intender is not such a fanciful example. The mammalian visual cortex contains cells that function as edge detectors and as line orientation detectors (Hubel and Wiesel, 1979). A cell that fires in response to visual edges is, in effect, a VISUAL-EDGE-STATUS intender. When such a cell is activated, we get a primitive attitude with the content that a visual edge is present. We should not infer from this that we have a representation of visual edges, but only of presence.

Once again, it is the idea that having an attitude that p is standing in a relation to a representation that p that is at fault. And it is worth reiterating how bad the fault is. A doctrine that collapses the distinction between attitude content and representational content will collapse the distinction between the content of a representation and the content of its applications, leaving no room for the distinction between targets and contents, and hence no room for the notion of representational error. Where there is no possibility of representational error, there is no representational content either.

Problem 3: CT and Explanation

So much for internal criticism. What really bothers me about causal theories of mental representation is that they throw no light whatever on the explanatory role of mental representation in cognitive theory. They thus fail to meet the Explanatory Constraint I identified in chapter 1; they don't explain why representation in the mind matters. They don't say, for example, why it should be theoretically significant that there is a symbol type in the mind that has the property that some of its tokenings are instances of a basic law in situ that tokenings of that type are caused by H, the property of being a horse. It is, of course, easy to see why detection matters, that is, why something regular should happen in response to H. But there is a great difference between seeing why detection should matter and seeing why representation should matter. CT is telling us that to represent H is to be implicated in a certain way in its detection. Causal theorists owe us a story about why having things in the mind that are implicated in a certain way in detection should be the key to understanding cognition.

Information

Whatever plausibility CT has as accounts of the explanatory role of mental representation, that plausibility derives from the idea that representations are indicators, viz. things whose occurrences (tokenings) carry information about the world. If you have a cell that fires when and only when you encounter a visual edge, then those firings carry the information that there is a visual edge present. And since it is evidently useful to have information, it seems plausible to suppose that representing is just indicating.[13] This idea was, I suppose, behind the fact that the cognitive

13. "Indication" is a technical term here: r indicates that x is $F = df\ r$ occurs when, only when, and because, x is F. When we speak of false indicators, we are speaking of things whose function it is to indicate but do not, or of things that are or were thought to indicate but do not.

revolution was led by something called information-processing psychology (Neisser, 1981).

Representation cannot be indication, as everyone knows, because there can be misrepresentation but not misindication: if *e* carries the information that there is a visual edge present, it follows that there is a visual edge present. But if *r* represents the presence of a visual edge, it does not follow that there is a visual edge present. Moreover, as Fodor (1990b) has emphasized, most uses of representations are not indicator uses (what Fodor calls labeling uses) anyway. The occurrence of a |cat| in |If cats were less selfish, they would make better pets| does not even have the function of carrying information about cats. Thus it is that causal theorists quickly concede that even correct representations of cats do not typically carry any information about cats at all.

Processing information is only useful if the processing preserves the information in some sense. It is therefore somewhat ironic that CTs typically link representation with information on the one hand and with a symbolic Language of Thought (LOT) on the other. (This is no accident, as we will see shortly.) LOT is supposed to do such things as allow Rover to get from |bell ⊃ food| and |bell| to |food|. And so it does. The trick, as Fodor likes to emphasize (Fodor, 1975, 1987), is that |bell| and |food| occur as constituents in |bell ⊃ food|. This means, among other things, that the meaning of |bell ⊃ food| is a function of the meaning of |bell| and of |food|. But, and this is the punch line, the information carried by |bell ⊃ food| is not a function of the information carried by |bell| and by |food|. Or, to make the same point from a different perspective, if it is a basic law that |bell & (bell ⊃ food)|s cause |food|s, then |food|s do not carry the information that there is food around, because something other than food can and does regularly cause correct tokenings of |food|, namely tokenings of |bell&(bell ⊃ food)|s, a point we met with previously.

Of course, as I've been at pains to emphasize, causal theorists don't think representing is carrying information. Still, as I also pointed out, CTs derive a lot of their plausibility from the idea that the basic case of representing is carrying information. It is this idea that makes it seem that CT is on to something that might be relevant to explaining cognition, for it is initially plausible to think that information might be relevant to explaining cognition. That is why it is a usefully purifying exercise to note that information and symbolic constituency don't mix. It is no good trying to make them mix by saying that a symbol's meaning that *x* is *F* isn't its carrying the information that *x* is *F* but its having the function of carrying the information that *x* is *F*, for the combinatorics of the symbol system will not give the symbol that function. Nor is it any good trying to make them mix by saying that a symbol's role in detection simply fixes its meaning, for then, as we saw above, one abandons altogether the idea that representing has anything to do with carrying information; one just adopts a trick that will associate the right meanings with the right symbols without telling us what representation is. The plain fact is that if you like the kind of combinatorics that symbolic schemes give you, informationland isn't where you should be looking for meaning.

The idea that computing over representations is information processing is thus abandoned at the very first step in constructing a causal-informational theory of content. And nothing remotely comparable, that is, nothing about what representation *is*, is ever put in its place. What we have instead is an attempt to attach the right meanings to the right symbols in any way that does not presuppose semantics or intentionality. And it is easy to get caught up in this game of *pin the meaning on the symbol*, because it is hard. A solution to this hard problem, even if we had it, might tell us nothing about what representation is and why it matters.

CT and the Tower Bridge

What story *can* advocates of CT and LOT tell about the relevance of content to cognition? I think the only story that can be told is the one that usually is told. It goes like this: In computational systems, representations affect processing in virtue of their form. Since there is a pretty good correspondence between content and form, generalizations couched in terms of content turn out to be pretty accurate. Since cognition is epistemic constraint satisfaction, and since epistemic constraints are stated in semantic terms, the target explananda of cognitive theory are effects stated in semantic terms. Hence, being able to track computations under their semantic interpretations allows us to see how a physical engine—a computer—can satisfy epistemic constraints.[14] There is a picture that goes with this story (figure 5.3). I called this picture the Tower Bridge (Cummins, 1989) because it reminds me of the Tower Bridge in London. The lower span is a sequence of computational events—the state transitions of a system as specified by a computer program. The upper span is a sequence of interpretations of events on the lower span—the computation seen under semantic interpretation. To the extent that content tracks computationally relevant form, content generalizations will turn out true. Or, to put it slightly differently, to the extent that content tracks computationally relevant form, computational systems executing the right program will be found, under interpretation, to exhibit cognitive effects.

14. This is the story I told in *Meaning and Mental Representation*, except that there I held that having a content just reduced to being implicated in a computation with the right sort of interpretation.

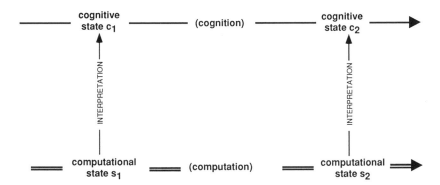

Figure 5.3
The Tower Bridge.

The Misalignment Problem
The Tower Bridge account of the explanatory relevance of content assumes a tight correlation between content on the one hand, and computationally relevant form on the other. There is, however, a serious threat to this correlation.[15] As Fodor has pointed out in criticizing two-factor theories (Fodor, 1987), there is nothing to prevent representations having conceptual roles that bear no relation to the contents dictated by the roles they (or their primitives, if they are complex) play in detection, since those roles do not determine any others. A representation that is identified as a |cow| by CT can have the conceptual role of a |horse|. But this is just a way of saying that content, as fixed causally, need not track form even approximately. Since the Tower Bridge account requires content to track form, and since the Tower Bridge account is the only account of the explanatory relevance of representation available to causal theorists, it follows that CT provides us with no reason to suppose that content has any explanatory relevance.

It is open to the causal theorist to reply that the form-content correlation is supposed to be contingent. Systems that typically reason with |cow|s as if they were |horse|s aren't impossible. But they can be expected to get into the kind of trouble that learning and evolution are likely to

15. Fodor (1994) points out that this correlation is threatened by two familiar sorts of cases. On the one hand, we have the so-called Frege cases—cases like "morning star" and "evening star" in which different forms have the same content—and on the other hand we have Twin Earth cases—cases in which the same form is alleged to have different contents. But it is arguable (Cummins, 1991b; Fodor, 1994) that these exceptions to form-content correlation leave the basic Tower Bridge picture intact if they are not pervasive. Fodor argues (1994) that there are mechanisms in play that work to keep them under control. The threat to the form-content correlation I will discuss is quite different.

correct or punish. Indeed, the fact that representationalist explanations work as well as they do can be cited as evidence that this sort of radical misalignment between content and form is relatively rare.

Plausible as this reply appears at first blush, I don't think it will stand scrutiny. Systems that typically reason with |cow|s as if they were |horse|s will no doubt encounter difficulties. But (1) systems that typically reason with |cow|s as if they were |ungulate|s, or better, as if they were |cow or apparent cow|s, can be expected to get into pretty much the trouble we actually do get into. So it looks as if the threatened misalignments won't be so rare after all.[16] Every case in which CRS and CT differ over a content assignment will be a case of form-content misalignment according to CT, and an embarrassment to its use of the Tower Bridge account of content relevance. And (2), it is unfair for the causal theorist to point out that treating |cow|s as |horse|s will lead to trouble, for whether things caused by cows are |cow|s is what is at issue. To keep things fair, the reply has to go like this: Representations Normally[17] produced by detectors in response to the property of being a cow will be treated as |horse|s only at a cost. This may be true, but it puts a different slant on things, for it invites us to suppose that it might be the detector that is at fault, rather than the reasoning, a possibility that CT rules out. To put matters graphically, suppose what the detector Normally produces in response to the property of being a cow is a model of a horse. (This is allowed, remember, for CT makes representation arbitrary.) Under these conditions, one might be excused for blaming the detector rather than the reasoning, especially if the system is designed so that models of horses have conceptual roles appropriate to |horse|s. To insist under these circumstances that a model of a horse is nevertheless a |cow| because of its role in detection seems just perverse.

Of course, if we stick to arbitrary symbols of the sort favored by LOT, as CT must, then any primitive representation may have any conceptual role, just as any primitive representation may have any role in detection (which, after all, is just a limited conceptual role). So, if you look at the situation through LOTish glasses, you are going to say that so far as the intrinsic properties of r go, there is no saying whether it is the detection or processing that is awry. What makes it appropriate to reason with r as if it were a |horse| is whether it is a |horse|, and since that can't be read off the intrinsic properties of r, what with r being arbitrary, it has to be read off something else. If you read it off its role in detection, you get the re-

16. It will not escape students of the game that a new form of the disjunction problem which has controlled so much of the dialectic surrounding CT returns here to haunt CT again.

17. Let representations Normally produced by detectors be representations whose production by detectors satisfies whatever conditions CT requires for content fixation.

sult that the processing is wrong. If you read the content of *r* off its conceptual role, you get the result that the detection is wrong. Either way, it is your theory of content that fixes where the problem is.

Notice how the commitment to arbitrary primitives drives the argument here. When you introduce something that looks nonarbitrary, like a model, the landscape shifts in a way that makes it difficult to see how CT could hope to avoid the misalignments between form and content that will undermine its appeal to the Tower Bridge. It is tempting to conclude from all this that, if you are a mental representation, it is your structure that matters, not your role in detection. Chapter 7 is a defense of the virtues of succumbing to that temptation.

CT and LOT

To see just how serious the misalignment problem is for CT, we need a kind of lemma, namely, that CT entails the LOT hypothesis. By LOT I mean the hypothesis that the mind's scheme of representation consists of a set of arbitrary primitives, together with complex representations formed from the primitives in a way that makes the content of a complex representation a function of the contents of its constituents and its logical form.[18]

CT pretty obviously implies that representations are arbitrary, that is, that their content is logically independent of their intrinsic properties, for if it is the causal connection to a property that gives a representation its content, then it cannot be any intrinsic properties of the representation that matter to its content. If you can build a horse detector at all, you can build one that responds to horses by tokening any symbol you like, and then that symbol will be a |horse| according to CT. A given physical detector might in fact produce a |horse| whose internal properties are not arbitrary, as cameras and human visual systems do, for example. But those properties are irrelevant to content, according to CT.

CT further assumes that only the meanings of primitive representations are fixed causally, and that all complex representations get their content via some sort of combinatorial semantics. To see this, imagine that a detector tokens a complex expression of the form $D \& P$, in response to a property μ, and that this is supposed to be a content-fixing detection. Now the contents of A and B will also be fixed by their roles in detection. But there is nothing to prevent designing a system that tokens D in

---

18. Although it is usually assumed, LOT doesn't entail that the set of primitives is finite. The usual argument for a finite set of primitives, namely, that each primitive has to be independently learned, doesn't apply here since LOT isn't learned. CT may entail that the number of primitives is finite since it may be that only finitely many representations could play the requisite role in detection. I've never seen an explicit argument for this, however.

response to ∂ and P in response to π, even though there is no relation whatever between ∂, π, and μ, for detectors can, and frequently do, operate independently of one another. It will follow that the meaning of D & P is not fixed by the meanings of its constituents, which is contrary to the hypothesis that it is a semantically complex expression. The only way to prevent this consequence is to stipulate that only semantically primitive expressions have their meanings fixed causally.

So, CT entails LOT.

The significance of this for present purposes lies in the fact that there are basically just three ways that arbitrary mental symbols can enter into cognitive explanations: (1) as *triggers* for procedures, (2) as *cues* for stored knowledge, and (3) as *constituents* of complex representations. The point can be brought out by a simple example. You are asked to go milk the cow. You make a plan to carry out this request. Among your early subgoals is the subgoal to find the cow. You decide to look in the barn. When you get to the barn, you walk around inside looking for the cow. You look in a stall, and token a |cow|. You get the stool and bucket, open the stall, go inside, and prepare to milk the cow.

So far, an arbitrary mental symbol will do fine, because the only role the |cow| in question plays is to get you to open the door to the stall. The |cow| simply *triggers* the next step in the plan. To get the door open, you need a representation of doors and latches, not of cows. But now that you've located the cow and are on the spot, you need to locate the udder. Here, something like a picture of a cow, an image, say, would be very helpful, whereas a mental word is totally useless unless it happens to function as a retrieval *cue* for some stored knowledge about cows. Faced with actually having to deal with a cow, the burden therefore shifts from the symbol to your stored knowledge, because the symbol, being arbitrary, tells you nothing about cows. So it turns out that it isn't because you have a representation of cows that you get the milking done, it is because you have a route—activated by a cue—to something else, some stored knowledge about cows. |cow|s play a role in stored knowledge about cows only as constituents of the complex representations—|cows have udders between their back legs|, for example—that are implicated in the possession of stored knowledge about cows.[19]

19. I don't think this should come as any real surprise to causal theorists, for I think the view is widespread that it is really stored knowledge that does the explanatory work anyway. But it is worth emphasizing that there is a big difference between appealing to the fact that one has a primitive mental symbol caused in detectors by cows, and appealing to the fact that one has a lot of knowledge about cows. The causal theory of representation commits one to the view that representations of cows don't tell you anything about cows.

Perhaps it isn't so bad that CT entails that the representations that get their meanings fixed causally have only an indirect role in the explanation of cognition, for there are always mental sentences to tell us about cows. But let's just be clear about what CT is committed to here: the view we have arrived at is that cognition is essentially theory application. All the serious work gets done by sets of sentences that are internal tacit theories (ITTs) about whatever objects of cognition there happen to be. As far as cognizing cows goes, your |cow|s really don't matter; it is your ITT of cows that does the work. For the sake of argument, then, so be it.

Now, if the Tower Bridge story is to work, there has to be a tight correlation between the content of an ITT and its computationally significant form. This means that the only form that can matter is the form that is implicated in the semantic composition of sentences from primitives. Any structure beyond what is required by a decompositional semantics has to be mainly inert. But—and here is the punch line—(1) theories, even construed as sets of sentences, have computationally relevant structure that is semantically irrelevant, and (2) it has been decades since anyone thought that complex mental representations were simply sets of sentences. Let's take these points in turn.

First, then, even sentence-set ITTs have computationally relevant structure that goes beyond what is involved in their semantics, namely:

- *Order*. The same sentences in different orders will interact differently with any process that involves serial search.
- *Redundancy*. Redundant theories will be larger, hence will take longer to search exhaustively, but may also be more efficient because cued recall provides multiple entry points.

These may look trivial, but their consequences can be profound, given limited resources. Whole ranges of problems that one system finds tractable will be beyond another that harbors what CT (but not CRS) takes to be a semantically equivalent theory.

Second, any recent data structures text will introduce the reader to many schemes for constructing complex representations whose interest lies precisely in the fact that they have computational properties that do not correlate with content as construed by CT and LOT. To get a feel for this, note that CT cannot accommodate representational schemes that are context-sensitive, and, because of this, cannot accommodate many interesting complex representations. Consider the scheme shown in figure 5.4 for drawing cartoon faces using elements in a "palette" of the sort familiar to users of computer graphics programs. The basic elements of this scheme, the circle, line, and curved line, have no meaning except in the context of a face (or some other meaningful picture or diagram). Since the faces are the only units that have independently specifiable contents, CT

Figure 5.4
Palette scheme for representing faces.

has to hold that each face is semantically primitive and has its meaning fixed causally, and that is surely unacceptable, since (1) it obliterates genuine semantic complexity—eyes, ears, noses, and mouths do get represented—and (2) this would make the set of primitives unbounded. By my lights, these facts alone should be enough to kill CT.[20]

The cartoon scheme is not symbolic. Since CT entails LOT, it comes as no surprise that CT cannot accommodate the cartoon scheme. Perhaps it should come as an unwelcome surprise to advocates of CT that many common symbolic schemes of the sort standardly found in orthodox computationalist models are also beyond the scope of CT. Consider, for example, the problem of navigating from a specified start point to a specified end point in a printed city map. An example city map is shown in figure 5.5. The system MATRIX uses a matrix of intersections to represent the city. Each entry is a list of available directions, with forbidden turns into one-way streets indicated by a minus sign. Thus, CITY$(1,3)$ = $(-w, -e, s)$, and CITY$(4,1)$ = (w, n, e, s). Start and end points are indicated by binding the beginning intersection to START, and the destination intersection to END. We may assume that MATRIX generates these matrices in response to geographical properties, for example, the property of having the geography of the map in figure 5.5. MATRIX uses a distance reduction algorithm to generate routes. MATRIX(CITY, START, END) can be thought of as a function that returns a sequence of the following instructions: GO RIGHT, GO LEFT, GO STRAIGHT.

A notable feature of the matrix representation is that rotations and transpositions of the matrix have no effect on the content of the repre-

20. It is difficult to simply dismiss schemes like this in view of the fact that they are obviously productive and systematic.

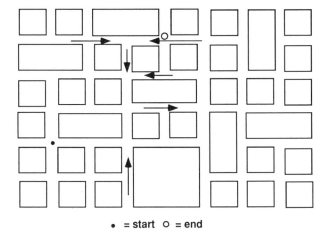

• = start   o = end

Figure 5.5
Schematic city map.

sentation. This is because intersection locations are strictly relative: actual coordinates don't matter; what matters are the locations of intersections relative to one another. It follows from this observation, however, that the scheme is molecular with respect to the representation of locations and distances (the main targets), since the accuracy in these respects of an intersection representation cannot be assessed independently of the whole set of intersection representations. And it follows from *that* that CT cannot accommodate the scheme MATRIX uses to represent cities. Yet MATRIX is just the sort of orthodox symbol-based computational system that is often supposed to exemplify LOT!

We could react to all of this by saying, "Well, maybe there is rather more misalignment between form and content than we thought. But we needn't fault CT and LOT. Instead, we could abandon the Tower Bridge story, or we could simply acknowledge that content explanations are rough and ready approximations." I think this really amounts to conceding the match to Stich (1983) by abandoning the Representational Theory of Mind for the Syntactic Theory of Mind. If that doesn't appeal to you, there is another option: Abandon CT and LOT. If

1. You think all that fancy structure cognitive scientists have been introducing into mental representations is semantically relevant,

but

2. You don't like CRS because you think that unused structure might still be semantically significant,

then

> 3. Perhaps you should take seriously the idea that it is the structure itself that determines content, independently of roles in detection or any other uses.

This is the motivation for chapter 7.

Indicators in Cognition

Nothing I have said here should be taken to imply that indication is not important in cognition. The point is simply that indicating an X—detecting one—does not require representing an X. This ought to be more or less obvious intuitively once we are free of the grip of CT. X, Y, and Z detectors might all do exactly the same thing in the presence of their targets because detectors are, in the standard and simplest case, devices that just "light up" in the presence of their targets. Neural detectors of line orientations all react in the same way to their target orientations, for example. What bit of Mentalese are we to suppose is tokened in all these cases? To avoid the conclusion—lethal to CT—that every detector tokens the same representation, advocates of CT will have to suppose that the representation in question is not the reaction of the detector, but the state of the detector. What makes the representations different is just the fact that they are states of different detectors. But if this is the line that defenders of CT take—and what else is there?—how can the system token these representations in nondetection uses? If you have to light up the cat detector every time you token a |cat|, you are going to be in serious trouble when it comes to what Hume called absent matters of fact, viz. nondetection uses.

The cure for this mess is to distinguish representations and attitudes. Lighting up a dog detector is a different attitude than lighting up the cat detector, but they are representationally indistinguishable. This, as I said, is more or less obvious to intuition unfettered by CT. Representation is supposed to give you a cognitive grip on a target, and detection, as we have seen, evidently gives you nothing beyond the brute capacity to pass control to something else that does have a grip.

Chapter 6
Atomism and Holism

A Pair of Distinctions

Holistic vs. Atomistic Schemes

A scheme of representation is holistic if the meaning of each basic semantic element in the scheme is internally related to the meaning of every other. It is diagnostic of holistic schemes that changing the meaning of existing basic elements (or adding or removing them) changes the meanings of the others. A scheme of representation is *atomistic* if the content of every basic semantic element is independent of the content of every other representation in the scheme. It is diagnostic of an atomistic scheme that adding to or subtracting from the expressive power of the scheme (by adding or subtracting a basic element or construction) does not change the meaning of the other basic elements.

On the face of it, some schemes in common use are atomistic, and some are holistic. Natural languages are atomistic in the sense lately specified: the meaning of "quark" is independent of the meaning of "unfair" on the grounds that adding the former to the language didn't change the meaning of the latter at all. Pictorial schemes, such as the cartoon face scheme described in chapter 5, are pretty clearly atomistic as well. Adding a new element to the palette, for example, a wavy line (good for hair and funny mouths), leaves previously available cartoons semantically unchanged.

By way of contrast, the familiar cartesian scheme for graphing functions is holistic. The primitives in this scheme are points located relative to a set of axes. Each point represents an element of a function, that is, the ordered pair corresponding to that point. The scheme consists of the axes (usually calibrated) and points and nothing else. To add primitives, that is, points, to a scheme like this you have to add an axis. Adding, for example, a third axis to a two-dimensional scheme changes the meaning of all the previously existing primitives. The point representing $\langle 1, 1 \rangle$ in the two-axis variation means $\langle \langle 1, 1 \rangle, 0 \rangle$ in the three-axis variation. Intuitively, the meaning of every primitive depends on its relations to others. The way to see this is to dub a point: call the point at $\langle 1, 1 \rangle$ "Sam". Now Sam represents the ordered pair it does solely in virtue of its location

Figure 6.1
Two palette schemes for constructing the same picture.

relative to other points; move it (relative to the origin, say) and it represents something else. Points couldn't get their meanings atomistically,
otherwise a point could mean $\langle 1, 1 \rangle$ irrespective of its position, which is
defined solely by virtue of its distance from other points.

Lexical Schemes vs. Molecular Schemes
By a lexical scheme I mean one in which the minimal semantic elements
are also the basic semantic elements. Molecular schemes are those in
which the minimal semantic elements are not the basic semantic elements,
because they have no meanings independent of their occurrence in a containing "complete" representation. The distinction can be made evident
by considering two kinds of palette scheme (shown in figure 6.1) of the
sort familiar to users of computer graphics programs. The lexical scheme
builds representations from a palette of independently meaningful elements (house, person, tree, street sign), whereas the molecular scheme
builds representations from elements (circle, curve, straight line) that are
meaningful only in context. Molecular schemes, in short, are those in
which the minimal semantic elements are context-sensitive[1]; lexical
schemes are those in which they are not.

1. As I understand "context-sensitive," a term is semantically context-sensitive just in case it
has a meaning only in context. This should be distinguished from cases in which context re-
solves ambiguity, or alters meaning (as in idioms).

Holism and Context Sensitivity

The kind of context sensitivity exhibited by molecular schemes should not be confused with holism. The idea behind holism is that the meaning of a representation in a holistic scheme is identified with that representation's relations to the other representations in the scheme, and this is quite distinct from the idea that the meaning of a representation depends on its context in a larger representation. To see the difference, note that we can add new basic elements to molecular palette schemes, thereby substantially increasing their expressive power without changing the meaning of any of the previously available representations. Such schemes are therefore atomistic in the sense defined above, but the minimal semantic elements (eyes, ears, nose, mouth) have no meanings out of context.

The tendency to confuse context sensitivity with holism is correlative with the tendency to see all representational schemes as "languages," and to confuse languages with theories. If you think that what the expressions in L mean is a function of the theories formulated in L, that is, if you think of the meaning of an expression in L as determined by its theoretical context, then you are thinking that expressions in L get their meaning from their roles in complex representations. If, in addition, you individuate languages semantically, then it will follow that which theories you hold determines which language you speak. So the idea that meaning is theory-relative, together with the idea that languages are individuated semantically, collapses the distinction between context sensitivity and holism. As we saw in chapter 4, you can think of use determining meaning in two ways: (1) meaning is determined by possible uses, that is, by, as it were, the theories that could be expressed in the scheme; and (2) meaning is determined by actual uses, that is, by the theories that one has actually accepted. If you think of things the second way, then you will see context sensitivity as tantamount to holism, for holism will follow from the assumption that the meaning of an expression is sensitive to theoretical context together with the assumption that meaning is determined by the theories one actually accepts.[2]

Notice that the definition given of holism by Fodor and Lepore (1992) is conveniently ambiguous between holism and the kind of context sensitivity encountered in molecular schemes. According to them, meaning is holistic when one thing's having a meaning requires that others do too. The curved line cannot be a nose unless something can be eyes and mouth, so this definition makes the cartoon face scheme holistic. But

2. Why is it the theories one accepts, rather than the ones one expresses, that matter? Because I might express T and $-T$, its denial (in the course of deciding between them, say). But the inferential role of a term w that would be fixed by its role in both T and $-T$ is of no interest.

"holism" in this sense, founded as it is on mere context sensitivity, doesn't even *seem* to entail the sort of meaning incomparability with which they tax holism generally.[3]

Tail Wags Dog

If we take the existence of both holistic and atomistic schemes at face value, as I think we should, then we should view with suspicion any theory of representational content that entails that representational content *itself* is intrinsically holistic or intrinsically atomistic. We have already had occasion to note that conceptual role semantics (CRS) entails that content is holistic,[4] and that causal theories of content (CT) imply that content is atomistic. We are now in a position to see that there is something odd about this result: whether a scheme is holistic should depend on the structure of the scheme, not on our theory of meaning. CRS will make every scheme holistic, regardless of its structure, just as CT will make every scheme atomistic, regardless of its structure. Surely the tail is wagging the dog here: meaning is holistic in holistic schemes of representation, whereas meaning is atomistic in atomistic schemes of representation. To adopt a theory of meaning that makes graphical schemes atomistic or the cartoon face scheme holistic is to mistake the role of a theory of meaning.

It is an objectionable feature of current accounts of representational content that they make the holism or atomism of content a feature of content, rather than a feature of a representational scheme. It would be desirable to have a theory of representational content that applied to both holistic and atomistic representational schemes, one that made content

3. Note that holism in the sense of Fodor and Lepore (1992) might well be true of attitudes. Since, on standard views, belief is functionally defined by its relation to other attitudes, including desire and intention, you cannot have beliefs unless you also have desires and intentions. It looks like functionalism entails that you cannot have just one attitude. Maybe you could have just one belief; it is hard to say, because beliefs are hard to count. But suppose the capacity for modus ponens is required for having beliefs on the grounds that it is, among other things, required to mediate the constitutive relations with desire. And suppose modus ponens takes more than one belief to apply ($p \supset q$ and p as opposed to $(p \supset q)\&q$). It wouldn't follow that you couldn't have a single belief, but it would follow that a single belief could never function as a belief.

However that may be, holism *in their sense* about beliefs wouldn't begin to entail that the mind uses a holistic representational scheme *in my sense*, nor would it begin to entail that meaning is holistic.

4. CRS entails more than that mental representation is holistic, for it also entails that altering inferential or other processing capacities will engender a global shift in meanings. Enforcing an internal relation between representational content and inferential capacity is one way to guarantee holism, but you can have holistic schemes without entangling your contents in your inferences.

holistic in holistic schemes and atomistic in atomistic schemes. What makes this an attractive goal is simply that it seems possible to semantically compare different representational schemes. When we argue that there are propositions that can be expressed symbolically that cannot be expressed pictorially, for example, propositions about triangularity, we are presupposing that both symbolic and pictorial schemes express propositions. This rather interesting and apparently meaningful claim would be trivialized by the doctrine that sentences and pictures don't have contents in the same sense. It would also seem incompatible with Descartes' important discovery that graphs (holistic) and equations (atomistic) can represent the same functions.

This argument deserves a quick summary for emphasis: If we assume (1) that representational content is holistic in some schemes and atomistic in others, and (2) that 'representational content' applies univocally to holistic and atomistic schemes, then we must reject any theory of content that makes content intrinsically atomistic (e.g., CT) or intrinsically holistic (e.g., CRS). Assumption (1) seems a very obvious fact of life, once we shed the blinders provided as standard equipment with current theories of content. Assumption (2) is entailed by the possibility of semantic comparisons between holistic and atomistic schemes.[5] So we should reject any theory of content that makes content intrinsically holistic or intrinsically atomistic. Indeed, we should reject any theory that makes content intrinsically *P* for any property *P* that varies across representational schemes.

More Leverage for Tails?

Maybe you could get the tail to wag the dog after all by arguing (a) that mental meaning is atomistic or holistic (pick one) on the grounds that the scheme of mental representation is, in fact, atomistic or holistic (pick the same one), and (b) that all representation is parasitic on mental representation.[6] If this could be made to stick, I suppose it would make content

5. But haven't I just been agreeing with Haugeland that pictures and sentences are incomparable?

No. That's not Haugeland's point, and it's not mine either. I've been agreeing that they are incommensurable, which is quite a different matter. The point about the incommensurability of sentences and pictures is that, for example, a picture cannot have the content *that something is triangular*, but can have other contents. As noted in the text, this point evidently presupposes that "Sentences and pictures both have representational contents," is not a pun.

6. Early Oxbridge variation: *Language* is atomistic or holistic (pick one), and all meaning is parasitic on language. I'm not even going to consider this. To believe it, you have to think either that apes and dogs don't have representing minds, or (even more silly) that their representing is somehow dependent on ours (as "conserving causes" perhaps?). And you have to think that pictures and maps represent only because words do. If you think any of these things, you think cognitive science is far too screwed up to waste time on its foundations.

atomistic or holistic *au fond*. But it can't be made to stick, I think, and that for two reasons.

First Reason

To show that meaning itself is, say, atomistic, it isn't enough to show that all representation is parasitic on an atomistic scheme of mental representation. One would have to show as well that mental meaning *has* to be atomistic. One has to rule out the possibility of intelligent aliens whose scheme of mental representation isn't atomistic. I can think of only two ways to argue that mental representation *must* be atomistic (or holistic). You could try to argue that meaning generally is atomistic (or holistic), and hence that mental meaning is. But that clearly begs the question at issue. Or you could try to argue that nothing counts as a mind unless it can be X, and that only a system that uses an atomistic (or holistic) scheme could be X. This strategy—I'll call it the essential feature strategy—requires a little more discussion.

Here is an argument that appears to have the relevant form.[7]

1. Nothing counts as a mind unless it is *productive* and *systematic*. (A mind is productive in the intended sense just in case it can have an unbounded number of content-distinct thoughts.[8] It is systematic in the intended sense just in case it cannot think that Rab unless it can also think that Rba.[9])

2. But the productivity and systematicity of thought require a productive and systematic representational scheme. (A scheme is productive just in case it can express an unbounded number of distinct contents. It is systematic just in case it can represent a content of the form Rba if it can represent a content of the form Rab.)

3. Only schemes that exhibit "classical constituency" (cc) are productive and systematic. (A scheme exhibits classical constituency in the intended sense if tokening *r* requires tokening all of its constituents.)

7. No one, to my knowledge, has actually tried this on. But all the pieces are there. I am certainly not attributing any such argument to Fodor, for example, whose discussion of systematicity has a quite different end in view.

8. The usual idealization away from resource constraints is assumed.

9. This formulation presupposes that contents have forms individuated by their constituent structures, which is hardly uncontroversial. The usual way of putting the matter is hopeless, however. It is usually said that a mind is systematic just in case you cannot think a thought of the form Rab unless you can also think a thought of the form Rba. This is hopeless because it assumes that thoughts themselves have forms individuated by constituent structure, and that is the conclusion we are invited to draw from the premise that thoughts are systematic. More of this shortly.

4. Only atomistic schemes exhibit cc.
5. Therefore, mental representation must be atomistic.

To defeat this line of argument, it suffices to produce a scheme of representation that is holistic but also productive and systematic. The standard scheme for representing functions graphically fills the bill. It is obviously productive since it can, for example, represent all the constant functions of one argument. It is obviously systematic since whenever the scheme can represent $f(x, y)$ it can represent $f(y, x)$.[10] So the argument fails because premise 3 is false.[11]

This objection, however, evidently does not generalize, depending, as it does, on the specific character of X, the mental property alleged to require an atomistic scheme of representation. What I want is a generalizable objection, an objection that blocks the essential feature strategy by showing that there is no property X that minds have necessarily and that requires an atomistic scheme of mental representation. It is pretty clear that I'm not going to get what I want. But we can begin to see how difficult it is going to be to make the essential feature strategy work by examining another (and better) attempt to apply it.

1. Nothing counts as a mind unless it is capable of incremental learning. (Learning is incremental in the intended sense if it adds to, but does not alter, what is already known.)
2. If mental representation is holistic, then learning something new, since it involves acquiring a new belief, alters the contents of all one's beliefs.
3. Hence, mental representation must be atomistic.

As it stands, premise 2 won't do, because, as we've had occasion to note, even CRS, in its functionalist guise, doesn't entail that adding (or subtracting) *attitudes* changes contents. In general, holistic schemes are not semantically sensitive to which representations are actually applied, hence not sensitive to which attitudes one actually has or acquires or loses. Holistic schemes are semantically sensitive to the addition or subtraction of *representational* resources, not the addition or subtraction of epistemological resources (like knowledge or belief). Since representing something new—something one has not represented before—typically doesn't require adding to the expressive power of one's representational scheme, premise 2 is false.

To fix the argument, we need a kind of learning that requires adding to the expressive power of one's representational scheme. For all I know,

10. Where both exist, of course. A similar restriction applies to the systematicity of thought: you cannot think the thought that Rab if there is no proposition that Rab.
11. So is premise 4, by the way, as the graphing scheme also shows.

there may be learning like that—Piaget thought so. But, and here is the kicker, anything that has a prayer of fixing (2) is going to undermine (1). Maybe there is learning that requires the expansion of representational expressive power, but what reason could we have to think that such learning is a *necessary* feature of all minds? Pretty much everyone seems agreed these days that expressive power is (a) pretty much fixed, and (b) changes as a function of maturation and trauma, not learning. Pretty much everyone could be wrong, but, if they are, their mistake surely isn't *metaphysical*. Surely God, or AI, might one day create a mind whose initial representational scheme is as powerful as ours ever gets.

I think there is a Real Pattern here that is bound to emerge in any attempt to employ the essential feature strategy: any argument that the crucial feature requires an atomistic scheme of representation is going to undermine the claim that it is essential to mind. This is because, on the one hand, whether a scheme is atomistic or holistic is independent of both its expressive and causal powers, and, on the other hand, arguments that a feature essential to mind requires a certain kind of representation are bound to turn on an appeal to expressive or causal powers. There just isn't going to be any place for the atomism/holism distinction to get a purchase.

I've been running the discussion of the essential feature strategy on the assumption that the goal of the strategy is to show that mental representation is atomistic. But we are now in a position to see that the strategy is likely to fare no better when the goal is to show that mental representation is holistic. The independence of a scheme's expressive and causal powers from its atomism or holism is going to hamstring the strategy no matter who is running it.

Second Reason
The issue, recall, is whether one could argue that meaning is atomistic or holistic *au fond* on the grounds that mental representation has to be, and that all other representation is parasitic on mental representation. We've just seen that the prospects are dim (though not closed) for showing that mental representation *has* to be atomistic or holistic. It is plausible, therefore, to suppose that it is contingent what structure our scheme (schemes) of mental representation actually has (have). If it really *is* contingent, then the theory of content should respect this fact by leaving it open. CRS and CT don't leave it open. If, like me, you think it is contingent what kind of representational schemes minds have, then you should be displeased with both CRS and CT on the grounds that they imply the contrary.

Conclusion

We would like, then, a theory of content that doesn't prejudge contingent questions concerning the kind of representational scheme minds do or can use. Unlike CRS and CT, an acceptable theory will not imply atomism or holism. An acceptable theory might, however, imply the presence of whatever causal or expressive powers (if any) are presupposed by whatever essential features of minds happen (as it were) to have.

Chapter 7
Representation and Isomorphism

Desiderata

Among the morals of the discussion so far is that we need a conception of representational content that is:

1. Distinct from targets
2. Distinct from attitude content
3. Independent of use or functional role
4. Neither holistic nor atomistic

Let's review each of these desiderata in turn.

Desideratum 1: The content of a representation must be distinct from its target
The central thesis of the foregoing discussion is that error is a mismatch between the content of a representation and the target of a particular use or application of it. A theory of representational content that does not explain how r's content is fixed in a way that is independent of how r's targets are fixed is bound to mishandle error.

Desideratum 2: The content of a representation is distinct from the contents of the attitudes in which it figures
When a representation r is applied to a target t and the resulting application is given a cognitive role, you get an attitude. The semantic content of an attitude is thus just the semantic content of its constituent application. The semantic content of an application of r to t is always, so to speak, that r represents t. Thus,

> Attitude content = application content
> = representational content applied to target

This equation makes it clear that identifying attitude content with representational content leaves no room for the contribution of targets to attitude content. But a theory that leaves no room for the independent contribution of targets leaves no room for error. A viable theory of representational content will therefore take care to maintain a clear distinction between the contents of a system's attitudes and the contents of its representations.

Desideratum 3: The content of a representation must be independent of its use or functional role
If we are to have a robust conception of error, we need a conception of representational content that makes the content of *r* independent of the way a system happens to use *r*, for error is using *r* to represent *t* even though *r* does not represent *t*. If using *r* to represent *t* makes *r* a representation of *t*, there can be no error. A meaning-as-use theory cannot work for mental representation. Perhaps it *is* possible to have a meaning-as-use theory for a shared language, for, in that case, we can distinguish individual use from general use and think of error as the gap between the two.[1] But an account of representational content adequate for psychology evidently cannot appeal to any analogous distinction. Nor, as we saw in the previous chapters, will a distinction between ideal (or Normal) use and actual use, or between actual and typical use, support an adequate conception of error. To create a space for error, we need a conception of representational content that makes the content of a representation independent of its use altogether.[2]

Desideratum 4: Representational content should be neither holistic nor atomistic
Some schemes of representation are holistic and some are not. It therefore cannot be a property of *meaning* that it is holistic or atomistic, so we must reject any theory of content that entails either holism (e.g., conceptual role semantics [CRS]) or atomism (e.g., causal theories).[3]

Preliminaries: Meaning and Meaningfor

Fundamental to what follows is a distinction between *meaningfulness* and *meaningforness*, and a correlative distinction between meaning and *mean-*

---

1. This is a notoriously unstable way to handle error even in the case of a shared language, for it does not allow for error in an ideolect. The standard move is to distinguish competence from performance: correct use of an ideolect is the use that would occur but for resource limitations, breakdown, and competition from other subsystems.
2. Perhaps it is worth reiterating that making any use of *r* meaning-fixing amounts to making that use of *r* infallible. But no use of any representation is infallible. At the very least, there can always be a slip of the computational wheels that results in applying *r* to a target it does not match.
3. The scheme (or schemes) of human mental representation might all be atomistic or all holistic. If you have the rather chauvinistic view that all meaning is ultimately parasitic on human mental meaning, then you could hold that "original meaning" is, say, atomistic. From this perspective, a theory of meaning that entailed meaning is atomistic would be defensible. But the blatant chauvinism of the perspective makes it pretty unattractive.

ingfor. Meaning (representation) is a two-place relation between a representation and a content; meaningfor is a three-place relation between a representation, a concept, and a cognitive system. A representation can be meaningful, that is, have a meaning, without having a meaningfor some cognitive system. And a representation can have a meaningfor a cognitive system that differs from its meaning.

R's meaningfor Σ is, intuitively, what Σ understands by *R*, or better, the *knowledge[4] that *R* activates or is associated with. For example, the word 'elevator' has a meaningfor me which consists of my *knowledge of elevators. By my lights, meaningfor should not be thought of as a *semantic* relation at all, but a cognitive one: When I understand *R*, *R*'s meaningfor me is not *R*'s semantic content—what *R* means—, but the chunk of knowledge that constitutes my understanding of the things satisfying that content. The cognitive notion of meaningfor is related to the semantic notion of meaning roughly as follows: If *R* means *elevator*, that is, represents the property of being an elevator, then *R*'s meaningfor me ought to be my *knowledge of elevators.

The concept of meaningfor has its natural home in thinking about language and communication. When we think of what a word means, it is natural (and correct, I think) to adopt the broadly Gricean (Grice, 1957; Cummins, 1979) perspective that what a word means is, or is a function of, what it communicates to speakers of the language to which the word belongs. What a word means, in short, is to be explained in terms of what it meansfor speakers of the language. When we think about language in this broadly Gricean way, then, the meaning is explained in terms of its meaningfor and not the other way around. Internal representations, however, are not of interest because of what they communicate; they are of interest because of what they represent. It is important, then, that we not think of the relation a system bears to its internal representations as like the relation we bear to, for example, maps. A map represents what it does quite independently of what it communicates to us or anyone else. But it also communicates something to us; that is, it represents a maze *to us.*

Many things that represent the maze will not represent it *to us*—will not communicate the shape of the maze to us—because they are not tokens of communicative types we are familiar with. Indeed, many things that represent the maze will not represent it *to* anyone or anything, that is, will not communicate the maze's features to anyone or anything. Because our models of the role of a representation in enabling intelligent behavior tend to be things like reading a map, we tend to think of representations

---

4. *Knowledge is knowledge as this term is used in psychology and artificial intelligence. It need be neither true nor justified, and it need not be conscious or accessible to consciousness. It is what philosophers typically call belief.

as useful because of what they communicate to their users. It takes little reflection, however, to see that this is not the model we should have in mind when thinking about internal representations. Reading a map is a sophisticated cognitive performance; it is just the sort of thing we want to explain by appeal to internal representations. Internal representations are not useful because of what they communicate: They do not communicate anything, that is, they do not represent anything *to* their users. Internal representations are useful because of what they represent, that is, because of what they mean, not because of what they meanfor. Thus, the fact that what something represents *to us* is not the same as what it represents *to something else* should not tempt us to relativize representational content to users or consumers; it should lead us to distinguish the semantic concept of representation (meaning) from the cognitive concept of meaningfor.

The distinction between meaning and meaningfor is obscured by a kind of ambiguity in the use of the word 'concept' in the cognitive science literature. My concept of an elevator is taken to be

1. My cognitive grip on elevators, a cognitive structure that is, or at any rate, organizes my *knowledge of elevators
2. A mental representation—an |elevator|[5]

Number 1, I think, is the majority view of concepts: to have the concept of an elevator is to have basic knowledge of elevators. Having a structure of attitudes—beliefs, intentions, plans, and so on—that constitutes basic *knowledge of c counts as having a concept with the content c. If you ask someone what an elevator is, they might say something like this:

Imagine a little room like a closet that moves up and down in a vertical shaft in a building. You get in on one floor, and the thing moves up or down to other floors where you can get off. Faster and easier than stairs. I think it is done with pulleys. Modern ones are controlled with buttons inside, and you can call it with a button by the door leading to it on any floor.

And they draw a diagram like the one in figure 7.1. This much, I think, would be plenty in ordinary life or a psychology experiment to establish that the "subject" has the concept of an elevator. And it would be enough precisely because it would demonstrate basic knowledge of elevators. So

5. There is a third use of 'concept' that is less common, but should be mentioned: "sentences express propositions, terms express concepts." Here, concepts are semantic contents, abstract objects on a par with—indeed typically constituents of—propositions, hence not psychological things at all, but the sort of thing that is specified by a satisfaction-condition in the way that a proposition is specified by a truth-condition.

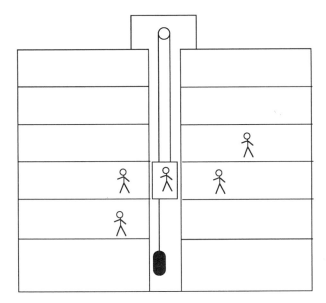

Figure 7.1
Schematic drawing of an elevator.

it seems clear that one can be said to have a concept of *F* in virtue of having a basic knowledge of *Fs*. We have already seen, however, that one can
have attitudes about elevators without being able to represent elevators.
It follows that one can be said to have the concept of an elevator even
though one cannot mentally represent elevators: (1) does not presuppose
(2).

It is worth pausing to let this point sink in. Knowledge structures are
not mental representations, not even complex mental representations.
They are organized attitudes. When one thinks of concepts, however, one
is typically thinking of a knowledge structure. To have the concept of an
elevator or horse is to have an organized knowledge structure about elevators or horses. Investigating concepts in this sense is not investigating
mental representations, except rather indirectly. A failure to notice this
point can make CRS seem spuriously plausible. One notes that one cannot
be said to have the concept of assassination if one does not know that assassinated people are dead, and concludes correctly that whether or not
someone has the concept of assassination depends on what they know.
But if you think that concepts are mental representations, you will think
you have concluded that whether or not someone has a mental representation of assassination depends on what he or she knows, and that is CRS.
That conclusion doesn't follow, however. It depends on an equivocation

on two senses on 'concept', an equivocation that goes unnoticed unless one pays attention to the distinction between attitudes and representations. Knowledge structures, like one's concept of an elevator, are not representations.

It should now be easy to see how sloppy use of 'concept' encourages the assimilation of mental representations to knowledge structures, and hence the assimilation of meaning to meaningfor. Good philosophy of mind must resist this assimilation, however, for it undermines the explanatory interest of representation. Representation is supposed to explain cognitive capacities, and therefore cannot presuppose them. If we understand the semantic notion of representation in terms of the cognitive notion of meaningfor, our understanding of representation does presuppose cognition, for meaningfor is a cognitive relation. Meaningforness is a cognitive phenomenon of just the sort that the notion of mental representation is supposed to help explain. Our target is therefore *meaning*, not *meaningfor*.

The Picture Theory: Preview

The theory of representational content I favor is a version of the "picture" theory. The main features of the account are these.

1. The most basic conception of representation—representation proper —is the conception one finds in mathematics. Representation is a relation between two structures[6] **R** and **C** such that **R** is said to represent **C** just in case **R** and **C** are isomorphic. We could call this notion of representation *m*-representation to acknowledge its mathematical origin, but I am going to call it representation *simpliciter* because I want to air the radical thesis that things whose semantic properties are not grounded in isomorphism don't *represent*, properly speaking, at all: they have meaningfor but not meaning.

2. According to (1), only structures represent, since only structures can be related by isomorphism. Many things, notably the expressions of a natural language, have semantic properties without being representations. These typically have semantic properties *conventionally*. For instance, "stop" means *stop* in English because speakers of English are parties to a convention according to which "stop" means *stop*. Since expressions in a language can be thought of as structures, languages are representational schemes. But the conventional meaning of a linguistic expression, that is, its meaningfor its users, is only coincidentally related to its representational content. You can understand a linguistic expression without having

---

6. A structure is a set of things and a set of relations on them. For example, the natural numbers together with the relation GREATER-THAN is a structure.

a clue about its representational content (if any). Representational content is irrelevant to the conventional meanings (i.e., meaningsfor) that expressions have in natural languages, just as conventional meaning is irrelevant to the content of mental representations. From the point of view of linguistics, the representational content of a natural language expression is as irrelevant as the chemistry of the ink in which it is written.

3. Mental representation is representation grounded in isomorphism. Since mental representations are not convention-governed, part of the motivation for my theory is that representation based on isomorphism is not conventional and can be shown to meet the desiderata listed in the previous section.

4. Construing mental representation in terms of isomorphism underwrites the explanatory role of mental representation in contemporary theories of cognition. No other conception of mental representation appears to do this.

Isomorphism and Cognitive Explanation

Representations as Proxies
One way to see the relevance of representation to cognition is to note that representations would have a clear explanatory role if they could be thought of as representatives of, or proxies for, the things they represent. To get a feel for this idea, I want to tell a kind of historical fable.

Once upon a time, it seemed that it was impossible to know a changing world. One went around snapping pictures of the world and storing them up in a photo album called Memory. But the pictures rapidly became outdated. Theatetus grew, fall succeeded summer, balls rolled down inclined planes, and the river flowed on. A changing world, it seemed, is just not the sort of thing one can know for more than a disappearingly small instant. Numbers, on the other hand, and essences, never change. So mathematics could be known, and, though Theatetus couldn't be known, the Form of humanity could be known, and maybe even the property of being Theatetus. So Aristotelian science is, perhaps, possible.

Elegant as this idea is, however, it doesn't seem so much a solution to the problem as an attempt to change the subject. So everyone was pleased and relieved when Galileo came up with a better idea. If you could just discover the principles of natural dynamics and express them in mathematical form, then you could compute updates of outdated world pictures. If you knew where the ball was on the inclined plane at a given moment, and its velocity at that moment, and the angle of the plane, you could compute its current position and velocity. For this to work, of course, one's representations of the world have to be the sorts of things that can be the objects of computational processes, so mathematics stayed at center stage, though now for a different reason. This sort of approach is harder to apply to Theatetus, the seasons, and the river, but perhaps that is just a matter of resource constraints. Humans, being finite, cannot know everything, after all. According to Laplace, God could work it all out from the instantaneous positions and momenta of all the particles in the universe. Of course, this seems to be a story about how God, or scientists, or maybe the institution of science, could know a changing world. But it was not long before the wise men at the East Pole (Dennett, 1986) conceived a way to apply the idea to all cognition: on the assumption that comparable, though perhaps cruder, representations and laws (now called rules) and the computing machinery are *in each of our heads*, though, doubtless without our awareness, we would not only be able to see ahead and plan, but to see the back sides of things and hear the source of a noise. Anything we can compute from current theory and data (rules and representations) can be known. So, inferring to the best (best because only) explanation, whatever we do know is computed from preexisting rules and representations. Thus was born what Haugeland (1985) calls GOFAI (good old-fashioned AI). Of course, we can't operate like Laplace's God. We have to settle for approximations cobbled together mainly by a mess of special-purpose modules evolved to do the job well enough to have kept the species alive *so far*.

For GOFAI to work, transformations effected on the representations by internal computations must mirror transformations effected by nature on what is represented. The mind, in short, must be able to simulate nature. So, the inner psychological dynamics defined over representational states had better be isomorphic to the outer dynamics of the "task domain," that is, of that bit or aspect of the world one is said to cognize. When that happens, a representation *r* in the head is a proxy or representative to the mind of the thing represented, for it will behave in the mind in a way analogous to the way the thing it represents behaves in nature, being disciplined by the computational laws of the mind as the thing represented is disciplined by the laws of nature.

This is the story that motivates the account I gave in *Meaning and Mental Representation* (Cummins, 1989): If a system Σ disciplines its representations in a way that mirrors the way nature disciplines the things represented, then Σ is in a position to simulate its target domains, and hence to cognize them. What I find compelling about this story is that the idea of representations as proxies in the mind's economy of things in nature's economy seems to give us a clear picture of representation's explanatory relevance to cognition. Having a representation of a ball on an inclined plane, on this account, is having something that will "behave" in the mind in a way analogous to the way a ball on an inclined plane behaves in nature. Hence, having a computational grip on the representation is having an epistemological grip on nature that allows one's knowledge to extend way beyond the information contained in the flux of one's sensory surfaces and its stored record (if any). A good theory of mental representation ought, above all else, to meet what I called the Explanatory Constraint in chapter 1: it ought to make us understand how appeals to the capacity to represent could explain cognitive capacities. And that is just what the representations-as-proxies story seems to do.

Unfortunately, the story as I've just told it, and as I told it in *Meaning and Mental Representation*, is no good. It is no good because it is a use theory, a version of functional role semantics, and therefore falls prey to the critique of CRS in chapter 4. There is, however, a way of holding on to the attractive idea of representations as proxies while avoiding CRS, and that is to adopt a version of the "picture theory" of meaning, that is, the theory that representations are isomorphic to what they represent. This theory retains the idea that elements or aspects of a representation stand to one another as elements in the thing or situation represented stand to one another, while rejecting the idea that it is the mind's processing that structures the relations between elements in a representation. In the maps we considered in chapter 5, for example, the blocks stand to the spaces between them as the buildings stand to the streets, and this is what makes it possible to assess the accuracy of a map independently of how it is used. I shall call meaning *intrinsic* when it is independent of use in this way. What blinded me for a long time to the possibility of intrinsic meaning was the general obsession with symbols. Symbolic schemes, consisting as they do of arbitrary semantic primitives, are not intrinsically meaningful. In a symbolic scheme, functional role is the only source of the kind of structure that the proxy story requires. Symbols cannot, as it were, discipline themselves, so whatever discipline they exhibit is imposed by the processes that use them. But in many nonsymbolic schemes, such as maps, representations are structured internally in a way that allows us to tell the proxy story without reference to functional roles.

Maps are isomorphs of the things they map, and this is what allows us to say, for example, that the blocks are proxies or representatives of the buildings, and the spaces between the blocks are proxies or representatives of the streets. What isomorphs share is structure, so the idea behind the Picture Theory of Representation (PTR) is that to represent something is to have its structure. It is having the structure of the world at one's computational fingertips that is crucial to cognition.[7] The structure that is crucial to cognitive explanation is extrinsic to symbols, but internal to such things as maps. This is why, as I shall argue later, symbols are primarily in the communication business while maps and the like are primarily in the representation business. It is also (and equivalently) why reference isn't representation. You can refer to the world and all its parts

7. Thus, PTR does revive the ancient idea that to know a thing is to have something in your head that has the same form as the thing known.

without harboring any information about it at all. That is why a theory of reference isn't going to help us understand cognition in the way that a theory of representation is supposed to.

Representations as Re-presentations
There is another way of seeing how isomorphism underwrites the explanatory interest of mental representation, and that is to see how construing representation as isomorphism allows us to see a close analogy between representation and perception.

Imagine a model car that has cogwheels on the rear axle so that when it moves forward a cogged plastic card is drawn by the axle through the car, parallel to the ground. In the card is a slit, and a pin on the tie rods that control the steering passes through the slit. As the car moves forward, the pin is moved side to side by swerves in the slit, directing the car (figure 7.2). If we put the car in a maze, we can design a card that will allow the car to negotiate the maze successfully. Such a card will be a kind of map of the maze, or, rather, of a successful path, for there will be an isomorphism between the slit and the successful path in question.

The tie-rod pin that senses the slit in the card could instead be driven by an arm that senses a groove in the floor of the maze that runs along the successful path. That sensing a groove in the maze floor should allow the car to negotiate the maze successfully is no surprise. That sensing the slit in the card should accomplish the same thing is also no surprise on the assumption that the slit and groove are isomorphic, for, in that case, the slit in the card is just a proxy for the groove in the floor. Sensing the representation is just as good as sensing the environment, provided the representation is accurate.

In this story, having one's actions guided by a representation is just like having one's actions guided by the environment. Since it is obvious why being guided by the environment is useful, it is obvious why being guided by a representation is useful. In a more sophisticated system, an isomorph of a domain would allow one to explore that domain in absentia. Representation-as-isomorphism—the picture theory—allows one to understand why meaning matters without identifying meaning with functional role. This contrasts sharply with causal theories which entail that what matters is form, not meaning, and which individuate forms by functional role.[8]

---

8. The form of a primitive symbol is just its type. Form matters in symbolic systems because different types have different functional roles, that is, because they are processed differently. Causal theories associate meaning with form in a way that ignores the actual causal role of form everywhere but in detection. In such theories, meanings are simply tacked on to forms in a way that robs meaning of any significant explanatory role to play. This was the central moral of chapter 5.

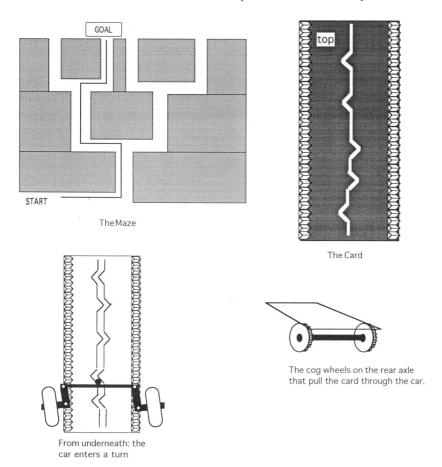

GOAL

top

The Maze

The Card

The cog wheels on the rear axle
that pull the card through the car.

From underneath: the
car enters a turn

START

Figure 7.2
The Autobot and a maze.

We can also see now how to deal with the problem of knowing a
changing world that motivated the historical fable that began this section.
We take a snapshot of Theatetus as a boy, but the boy grows to a man,
outdating our representation. The Galilean solution (slightly generalized)
was to fit Theatetus into a state space, and compute his future position in
that space. This solution is still available to PTR, but another related solution is available as well: "picture" the trajectory through state space, that
is, picture Theatetus expanding toward the future. Instead of changing
your representations, you can represent change. Instead of disciplining the
representations in a way that mirrors the dynamics you are interested in,
you can put the dynamic structure in the representation, that is, represent
the dynamics.

The picture theory, then, has much to recommend it.

• We can see our way clear to an account of how it satisfies the Explanatory Constraint.
• It makes meaning independent of use.
• It does not threaten a confusion of representational contents with targets or with attitude contents.

Let's see if we can give it a run for its money.

The Picture Theory of Representation

PTR rests on the idea that the representation relation is just the relation of isomorphism. This is the notion of representation we find in mathematics. When you prove what mathematicians call a representation theorem, what you prove is that a certain structure—a set of "objects" together with a set of relations defined on them—is isomorphic to some other structure. The idea is that there is a mapping between the two structures such that (1) for every object in the content structure C, there is exactly one corresponding object in the representing structure R; (2) for every relation defined in C, there is exactly one corresponding relation defined in R; and (3) whenever a relation defined in C holds of an n-tuple of objects in C, the corresponding relation in R holds on the corresponding n-tuple of objects in R.[9] Corresponding to the three clauses defining an isomorphism between structures are three sorts of things, other than the structure C itself, that can be said to be represented as well:

If a structure R represents a structure C, then

1. An object in R can represent an object in C.
2. A relation in R can represent a relation in C.
3. A state of affairs in R—a relation holding of an n-tuple of objects—can represent a state of affairs in R.

Note, however, that R does not represent C because the objects, relations, and states of affairs in R represent objects, relations, and states of affairs in C, but the other way around: things in R represent things in C because R is isomorphic to C. According to PTR, there is no such thing as an unstructured representation, except in the derived sense just introduced: an unstructured element in a representing structure R may be said to represent its counterpart in a represented structure C. We must be careful, then, not to think of the objects, relations, and states of affairs in R as in-

---

9. We get an isomorphic embedding of one structure in another if we relax the requirement that the mapping between structures be one to one and allow it to be onto.

dependent semantic constituents of R. PTR entails that every genuinely representational scheme is molecular in that the meaningful constituents of a structure are meaningful only in the context of some structure or other. As required, however, PTR is neutral between atomism and holism, since it evidently accommodates both the cartoon face scheme, which is atomistic, and the standard scheme for graphing functions which is holistic.

Multiple Isomorphisms
If PTR is to get off the ground, we must immediately face a problem that arises from the fact that isomorphisms, where they exist at all, are not unique. A structure R may be said to represent another structure C wherever R is isomorphic to C. In general, however, there are bound to be many isomorphisms, that is, many one-to-one structure-preserving mappings, between two structures if there are any. Hence, when R is isomorphic to C, there are many different ways in which each structure can represent the other. To see why this is a problem, recall the Autobot, the car that is guided by a plastic card with a slit in it. The obvious isomorphism maps left turns in the card's slit onto left turns in the maze, and maps right turns in the card's slit onto right turns in the maze. Call this isomorphism f. Now let m be a function that maps left onto right and right onto left, and define f^* as follows: $f^*(x) = f(m(x))$. Evidently, f^* is an isomorphism if f is. But it might seem, intuitively, that the card represents the correct path only under f, not under f^*, for, if we put the card in the car *upside down*, the car does not take the correct path but rather the mirror image of the correct path. (Since the groove goes all the way through the card, it can be used either face up or face down). If the card is a correct representation under f^*, should the car not run successfully with the card upside down? It seems that f and f^* cannot both specify the content of the card.

The invited conclusion is that specifying the content of a representation requires specifying a particular isomorphism. But if we say this, we will be abandoning the idea that the content of a representation is something intrinsic to that representation and independent of its use. For what, other than the way it is used, could make it the case that the card represents the maze relative to f but not relative to f^*? We could easily design a car that reacts to the upside down card just as the original car reacts to the right-side-up card. If we say that the card's content is specified by f in the original car, we shall have to say it is specified by f^* in its mirror twin. We shall then have to say that the content of the card changes depending on which car is using it. Since the independence of a representation's content from its use is the central requirement we have put on the theory of representational content in order to account for representational error, we must find another way to respond to the problem of multiple isomorphisms.

It is tempting to reply that f and f^* constitute different schemes, and that car1 and car2 just use different schemes. But if we say this, what will determine which scheme a system uses? The fact that car1 uses f rather than f^* could only be due to the fact that right swerves in the card's slit cause right turns in car1. But this, of course, assumes that the car is using the card correctly. So it is really *correct use* that fixes the car's scheme. That is why use can give us good evidence of content—when we have good reason to believe Σ is using its representations correctly—but cannot be constitutive of it. "Principles of charity" and the like in the theory of interpretation are what you get when you try to infer contents from targets, for contents match targets only in cases of correct use. A principle of charity has the effect of giving you the enabling assumption of correct use free of charge. This ought to raise suspicions: In philosophy, as in life, *there is no free lunch*. Anything that gets you the assumption of correct use free of charge eliminates the possibility of error by making any evidence of error better evidence for a different interpretation. Moreover, if we say use determines whether f or f^* is car1's scheme, we shall have to say also that use determines the content of car1's representations. For if use determines that car1's scheme is f rather than f^*, then use determines whether the content of a right swerve in the card is TURN RIGHT OR TURN LEFT.[10]

The existence of multiple isomorphisms is a problem because it seems to force us to the conclusion that specifying the content of R requires specifying a particular mapping, and it seems obvious that the only thing that could underwrite a choice of mapping is use or functional role, thus violating one of our central constraints on an adequate theory of content.[11] We thus appear to have a serious problem: if we say that specifying the content of a representation *does not* require specifying a particular isomorphism, then we will be left with no determinate notion of error (since what is error under f^* may be correct under f). But: no determinate notion of error, no determinate notion of content either. If we say instead

---

10. The idea that use determines scheme, hence content, is seductive in the case of the Autobot: put in the card and see if right swerves in the slit cause right turns. What could be simpler? Even if we didn't have ample prior reason to reject use theories, it is evident on reflection that the idea won't generalize, since, in a more complex system, right swerves in the card could cause right turns in car2 given compensating errors or malfunctions downstream.

11. Note that a causal theory is hopeless here, since there is no mechanism contemplated that could underwrite a causal connection between features of mazes and features of the slit cards.

We could, of course, add such a mechanism into the story, though it would greatly complicate matters. But it would be beside the point. *As things stand*, we have a perfectly respectable representational explanation of the car's behavior, and a causal theory has no prospect of helping us to understand *that* explanation.

that specifying the content of a representation (or scheme) *does* require specifying a particular isomorphism, then we seem to be forced to the conclusion that use determines content. But a central result of the argumentation to this point is that a clear conception of representational error requires a clear distinction between content and use. If use determines content, then there is no error, hence no content. Either way, it seems, we lose the notion of error, and hence the notion of content as well. What to do?

Let's begin with the Autobot example. The basic intuition I want to cleave to is that turning the card upside down does not change its representational content, any more than rotating a map changes *its* content. What changes, if anything, is the ability of the using system to exploit the representation properly. If your map is not properly oriented, you won't get to your destination, but *that is not the map's fault*. The correct information is there; you just do not or cannot exploit it. In general, we want to resist any formulation that forces us to infer misrepresentation from a mere failure to perform, since misrepresentation is compatible with— sometimes essential to—successful performance, and failed performance is compatible with accurate representation. In the Autobot case, the correct diagnosis of the car's failure to negotiate the maze is not that the card misrepresents a free path through the maze, but that the car cannot exploit that representation properly if the card is inserted wrongly. Given that the card does correctly represent a free path, the car will succeed only if it uses the card in the way specified by the interpretation function f.

"So," I hear someone asking, "on the card in question, does the circled portion of the slit [see figure 7.3] represent a right turn or a left turn?" Earlier, I warned against thinking of the elements of a representing structure as independent semantic constituents. We cannot settle what the card represents by settling first what its parts represent. Instead, we must look at the whole structure, determine what it represents, and then infer what its parts correspond to. The whole slit, then, represents lots of things. Among the things it represents is a free path through the target maze, and a free path through the mirror image of the target maze, as well as many bad paths through both. The circled portion is mapped onto right turns under certain isomorphisms, and left turns under others, and various other things having nothing to do with mazes and turns under still others. It is the fact that the target is *among* the things that the card represents that explains, *in part*, why the car succeeds in getting through the maze when the card is properly inserted in the car. But the qualification "in part" is important. Representational correctness isn't enough to explain success, as the case of the upside-down card vividly demonstrates. Even more obviously, perhaps, a printed picture of the maze represents a clear path through the maze, but is utterly unusable by the Autobot.

Figure 7.3
Driver card for the Autobot.

The plastic card can be used in two different ways.[12] In both cases, we wind up with the same attitude, viz. that the current path is P (where P is the property of having the structure that the free path and its mirror and so on share). But, and this is the crucial point, the fact that the attitudes have the same content does not imply that they are the same state. What the example shows is that we can have semantically equivalent representations, used in the same way, yet have different states. Indeed, it shows that we can have the same representation applied to the same target in the same box, yet have different states. Intuitively, what the Autobot case shows is that there is more to an attitude (though not to its content) than the representation's content, the target and the box. There are, in addition, lots of causally relevant physical facts about the representation that do not affect its content or what it is applied to, or which kind of attitude happens to be at issue, such as the orientation of the card relative to the car.

Lest this seem ad hoc, it is worth pausing to note that standard Language of Thought (LOT) stories are committed to the same point. Assume, for a moment, that beliefs are sentences in Mentalese written in the belief box. Each of us, of course, has a large number of beliefs. Assume that you and I have the same sentences written in our belief boxes: will it follow that we are in the same belief states? It will not. Assume that beliefs are accessed by searching the belief box sequentially. Then the con-

12. Perhaps it can be used in four ways, if it can be started at either end!

sequences of one's beliefs will depend critically on how the sentences in one's belief box are ordered. I may solve a problem more quickly than you do because the relevant information is near the top of my box, and near the bottom of yours.[13] One might object that this is not a case of the *same* representation in the same box having different consequences, since a set of sentences ordered in one way is not the same (complex) representation as the same set ordered in another way, though they have the same content.[14] Fair enough. But then one could argue with equal cogency that the card in the Autobot right-side up is not the same representation as the card in the Autobot upside down, though they have the same content. If different functional roles make different representations (though not different content), then orientation of card in the Autobot is analogous to order of sentences in the belief box. In both cases we have semantic equivalence in spite of difference in orientation or order, and in both cases we have representations that are deemed to be distinct on functional grounds.[15]

System Relativity

Unfortunately, it is tempting and common to move from the idea that the printed picture of the card is unusable by the Autobot to the conclusion that representational content is relative to a user or consumer. One begins with the reflection that the printed picture of the card, though it represents a path through the maze *to us*, represents nothing at all *to the Autobot*. It is a short step from this to the idea that what the plastic card represents *in/to the Autobot* depends on how it is put in: it represents one maze *to the Autobot* when it is put in "right-side up," and another maze when it is put in "upside down." This, however, is just the confusion of meaningfulness with meaningforness that I warned against earlier. Recall that we want to explain the latter, which isn't a semantic notion at all, in terms of the former, which *is* a semantic notion. We must, therefore, maintain a separation between what something represents from issues of usability by a system. To abandon this goal is to abandon all hope of articulating a notion of intrinsic representational content. We should cleave to this goal, for nothing less will provide conceptual space for a robust notion of representational error.

13. Of more interest, you may not solve the problem at all because the order in which you retrieve relevant information may lead you down a dead end.
14. Note that CRS entails that the two sets have different contents, since they evidently have different functional roles.
15. The point here is (or is an extension of) the one Fodor makes (1990). There he argues that the belief that Jocasta is eligible is the same belief, that is, a belief in the same proposition, as the belief that Oedipus' mother is eligible, but that they are yet different belief states, since we have different sentences in the belief box, and that difference *makes* a difference.

Keeping in mind, then, that we are not interested in what the slitted card meansfor the autobot, we can see our way clear to saying that both the printed picture and upside-down grooved card do indeed represent a clear path through the target maze, even though the Autobot cannot exploit the picture at all, and cannot exploit the upside-down card properly. We will avoid the idea that the card means one thing when it is "right-side up," and another thing when it is "upside down." In both cases, the information about the right path is "in there" all right; the only question is whether the Autobot can exploit it. It is crucial to a nonregressive understanding of the role of representation in cognition that we *not* think of this question—whether the Autobot can exploit a representation of a clear path—by analogy with the question of whether a child or a rustic or a tourist can exploit a good map of Paris when he or she is there. The latter question is, typically, a question about what the map can or will communicate to its user, and that is as much a question about the user as it is about the map. The former question is not a question about communication or understanding at all. Internal representations are not exploited by being understood. To suppose otherwise would render regressive any attempt to explain understanding (e.g., understanding a map) by appeal to exploiting internal representations. A system exploits an internal representation in the way a lock exploits a key: by being causally affected by its structure. Anything less austere than this will undermine the explanatory interest of internal representations altogether.

Grounding representation in isomorphism entails, as we have seen, that representational content is never unique. This non-uniqueness, however, does not undermine the explanatory value of representation in any way, for the explanatory work is done by the match (or mismatch) between content and target. The fact that a representation correctly represents many things other than the target has no tendency to devalue the important fact that it does (or does not) represent the current target, for it is the match or mismatch (or rather the degree of match) between target and content that bears an interesting explanatory relation to performance. The fact that PTR makes representational contents non-unique, therefore, presents no problem, provided it does not make representational content indiscriminate. A viable theory of content must have a system's representations making only such discriminations among that system's targets as is required to explain performance. But we should be wary of the assumption that differential success with two targets requires the capacity to represent those targets differently. What the Autobot case shows is that a system that cannot represent the difference between two targets— mirror mazes, for example—may yet perform differentially with respect to those targets. The Autobot successfully negotiates a maze but not its mirror even though it cannot represent the difference between them, because the consequences of an attitude that are due to its constituent representation are due to more than the representation's content.[16]

Representational and Communicative Content
What a map communicates to a given user or group of users, and what it represents, are evidently two different things.[17] Here are two cases to think about.

> 1. A map represents London, not Paris, but I think it is a map of Paris. What it communicates to me about the subway lines is not what it represents.
> 2. There is a convention among the members of a spy ring that a map of Paris means that one is being followed, while a map of London means that one is "clean."

In the second case, of course, it is *carrying* the map that has the communicative content, not the map itself. And so it is with communicative content generally: it is never the thing itself that has communicative content, but the act of issuing or displaying or tokening it. By contrast, a map represents what it represents independently of how anyone uses it. The fact that a map may be used—indeed, typically is used—to communicate what it represents should not obscure the fact that its representational content is not a function of its communicative content, as the examples show. An obsession with language has blinded us to this rather important fact. If our paradigm of the semantic is language, we will inevitably be led to suppose that what something means is a function of what it meansfor its users.

The temptation to relativize representational content to a using system is driven by a confusion of representational content and communicative content. When we think of what something represents *to* some system, we are thinking, literally or metaphorically, of what is communicated to it. We think of the role of mental representations in mediating intelligent behavior as like the role of a recipe book in generating cake-baking behavior. Recipe books must communicate something to us to succeed, and this requires that they be understood. Since the same recipe might be understood differently by different users, it makes sense to distinguish what the recipe meansfor you from what it meansfor me. But this is very much the wrong model of the role of mental representation in the mediation of intelligent behavior. Since it involves communication, reading a recipe is a

---

16. It is worth repeating that this is a point on which PTR and other theories of content do not differ. On every theory, causal properties individuate more finely than content, and consequences depend on causal properties.
17. I confess to having done my part to promulgate the confusion of representational content and communicative content (see Cummins, 1983, chapter 3).

sophisticated cognitive performance of the very sort that representation-alists want to explain by appeal to the capacity to represent. We cannot suppose that mental representations are in the communication business without undermining the goal of explaining cognitive capacities in terms the capacity to represent. In chapter 3, I imagined a CRSer arguing that we should not confuse what R_{P3} means *to us* with what R_{P3} means to the chess system that uses it. What R_{P3} means *to us* is just what R_{P3} *meansfor us*—what it communicates to us. R_{P3} doesn't meanfor anything to the chess system. This, however, doesn't imply that R_{P3} is meaningless. On the contrary, R_{P3} means P3. R_{P3} needn't communicate anything to any-body to represent P3; it needs to be isomorphic to P3. Moreover, that isomorphism is just what is needed for the system to interact appro-priately P3. Thus, the fact that we cannot infer the representational con-tent to R_{P3} from what it meansfor us should not tempt us to relativize the representational content of R_{P3} to the system that uses it. It should lead us to distinguish communicative content from representational content.

The tendency to confuse representational content and communicative content is aided and abetted by the availability of the form of speech, '*x* represents *y* to *z*', for this makes representation look like a kind of com-munication. It is just this confusion, I think, that underlies the widespread intuition that there is no representation at all in systems like the Autobot. For it seems quite obvious to most that the groove in the plastic card doesn't represent anything *to* the Autobot, though it does represent something *to us*. Similarly, it seems obvious to many that the data struc-tures in a computer don't represent anything *to the computer*, though they do represent something *to the programmer*. Replace the dangerous "repre-sents *to*" with "communicates to" and everything comes out right: the groove in the plastic card *does not* communicate anything to the Autobot, though it does communicate something to us. Similarly, the data struc-tures in a computer *do not* communicate anything to the computer, though they do communicate something to the programmer. But none of this has the slightest tendency to show that the groove in the plastic card doesn't represent a free path through the target maze or that data structures don't represent, for example, sets of propositions.

Left and Right: Isomorphic Targets
According to PTR, no mental representation can discriminate among iso-morphic structures, and this does set some counterintuitive limits on what can and cannot be mentally represented. Consider, for example, the differ-ence between left-handed and right-handed gloves. According to PTR, this cannot be represented. It doesn't follow, of course, that it cannot be known, or that one cannot have a concept of leftness and rightness, nor does it follow that left and right hands cannot be represented. What fol-

lows is only that the leftness of a left hand or foot, or of a left-handed glove or shoe, cannot be represented.

This is not, perhaps, as counterintuitive as it seems at first. I think we are inclined to think the leftness and rightness can be represented because there is a word in our language that means *left*, and another that means *right*, and we understand these words. But word meaning is, at bottom, meaning*for*, so the most we are allowed to conclude from the fact that we understand 'left' and 'right' is that we have concepts of leftness and rightness, not that we have representations of them. But it is not hard to tell a story about the concepts of leftness and rightness that does not imply the capacity to represent leftness and rightness. I learned which hand is my right hand by learning that the hand others told me was my right hand had a scar on the thumb. I remember having to look for this scar to determine which hand was my right hand. Eventually, I just knew, without having to look; I could tell in the dark.[18] Later, I added the knowledge that I write and throw with my right hand. To this basic knowledge one eventually attaches the knowledge that things like cars, animals, and other people have an intrinsic orientation, a way they are facing or moving, and that their right corresponds to my right when we face the same way (as in "Never mount a horse from the right"), that things without an orientation are assumed oriented as the speaker (as in "Look at the right side of the box"). My concept of right is just all this knowledge, viz. that my right hand is the one with the scar, the one that I write with and throw with, etc., and that the right side of something with an orientation corresponds to my right when we are oriented in the same way, that unoriented things are assumed oriented as the speaker, etc. Since I can have this concept, that is, all this knowledge, without having a representation of rightness or of leftness, it follows that I can know right from left, and distinguish right from left, without having a representation of rightness or leftness. This, of course, is armchair psychology, and should be evaluated as such. The main point is simply that understanding the words 'right' and 'left' requires, at most, having concepts of leftness and rightness, not representations of them, and that it is possible—even plausible—to explain the concepts of leftness and rightness without presupposing representations of them. Objection:

> Michelangelo's fresco on the ceiling of the Sistine Chapel represents God as reaching to Adam with His right hand. You can make God look left-handed by putting your slide of the famous ceiling in your projector backward, but then *you've got it wrong*. Similarly, when I

---

18. I suppose that the mechanism here involves associating 'right hand' with motor commands that move the right hand, and with perceptual analysis of stimuli from the right hand.

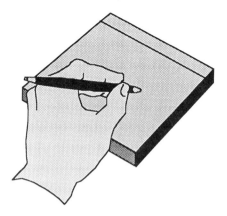

Figure 7.4
Left hand drawing.

imagine a left hand I form a different image than when I imagine a right hand. Similarly, when I see a right hand, I form a different percept than when I see a left hand. Surely these images and percepts count as mental representations that apply differently to right and left hands.

I could quibble about the underlying view of images here—viz. that they are like pictures—but I won't bother. Let's grant that they are like pictures, and ask whether a picture of a left hand represents leftness. Anyone, I suppose, can tell that the hand pictured in figure 7.4 is a left hand. But the obvious fact that pictures of left hands differ from pictures of right hands shows nothing to the purpose, since the issue is not whether we can recognize left hands, or pictures of them, but whether it is possible to represent leftness. I think it seems that pictures can represent leftness because we are inclined to confuse representing a left hand with representing its leftness. Pictures, we noted in chapter 5, can represent triangular things, but they cannot represent triangularity. From the fact that pictures can represent left-handed things—gloves, shoes, scissors—we should not infer that they can represent leftness. Indeed, the same argument that shows that pictures cannot represent triangularity—namely, that they cannot capture what all triangles have in common—shows that pictures cannot represent leftness: No picture can show what a left hand and left shoe have in common.

So: we have the concepts of leftness and rightness, and hence can understand 'left' and 'right'. But leftness and rightness cannot be pictured, though left and right things can be pictured. Since I see no compelling argument on the horizon for the view that leftness and rightness can be represented, it is no objection to PTR that it implies that they cannot. Moreover, what goes for leftness and rightness goes for differences among isomorphs generally. PTR implies that differences among iso-morphs cannot be represented, but it does not imply that they cannot be conceptualized, nor does it imply that they cannot be referred to or com-municated in words. PTR appears to be on relatively safe ground here, provided we maintain a distinction between representations and concepts, and between meaning and meaningfor.

Accuracy

We saw in an earlier chapter that the tradeoff between the degree of error with its seriousness is central to understanding cognitive adaptation. A theory of representation, then, needs to explain how error can come in degrees. Isomorphism does not come in degrees, so we have a problem here for PTR.

It is possible to hold out for the view that representational error doesn't come in degrees at all, on the grounds that it is concepts, not representa-tions, that can be more or less correct. Concepts, as I have been using the term, are more or less open-ended organized bodies of *knowledge, and one might hold that it is possible to explain what it is for a body of knowledge to be more or less accurate without resorting to the idea that representational accuracy comes in degrees as well. Here is how it might work. Think of each concept as a kind of minitheory. Theory accuracy, then, might be explained as follows: T is more accurate than T' if the pos-sible worlds in which T holds are closer to the actual world than the worlds in which T' holds.[19] I don't know whether or not this can be made to work, but I am going to assume it can for the sake of argument.

Having come this far, one might think this: If distances among possible worlds makes enough sense to define theory accuracy, it makes enough sense to define representational accuracy: R is more accurate than R' if the possible worlds in which R is satisfied are closer to the actual world than those in which R' is satisfied. The point seems to generalize: any way of defining theory accuracy will work for defining representational

19. Anyone who, like Fodor (1975, 1990b), thinks theories *are* representations is thereby committed to denying that theories can be more or less accurate, or to conceding that repre-sentations can be. If they accept the second horn of this dilemma, they are committed to meanings being more or less similar, for meaning similarity can evidently be defined in terms of theory similarity on the assumption that theories are representations: The content of T is more similar to the content of T' than to the content of T'' if the worlds in which T holds are closer to the worlds in which T' holds than to the worlds in which T'' holds. Not everyone is fond of distances between possible worlds, but these are not always the same people as those who are fond of denying that meanings are more or less similar.

accuracy.[20] So the thought is that we need not define "partial" isomorphism or anything comparable to get a graded notion of accuracy out of PTR. We simply say that r is an accurate representation of t to the extent that r's content is similar to t.

Tempting as this is, it should be resisted. According to PTR, representations can only represent structures. And while there may well be a graded notion of similarity for states of affairs or possible worlds, there is none, at least none as yet well defined, for structures. In any case, similarity on possible worlds or states of affairs, while secure enough perhaps, is surely not well understood. PTR would do well to find a way to stand on its own two feet. What is required is the notion of *how much* structure two structures have in common, or the notion of how similar two structures are. The notion that some maps, pictures, graphs, and so on are more accurate representations than others of certain targets is, I suspect, uncontroversial. What is not uncontroversial is that accuracy in such cases can be understood in terms of the degree to which two structures are alike.

I wish I had something clever and mathematical to say here, but I don't (yet). Swoyer (1991) suggests that relaxation of various constraints on his notion of structural representation will yield representation that is less than perfect in various respects. At this writing, I do not yet know whether this approach can be made to work as a general account of accuracy. Still, I am convinced that the problem has a solution. Consider the following examples.

1. As John Haugeland has pointed out to me in correspondence, different maps of Pittsburgh (which, Haugeland informs me, is not well mapped) might yet agree to a very large extent. Given three disagreeing maps, we might well be able to say whether A was closer to B than to C. Not that we could always do this reliably, but *sometimes* such comparisons would surely be uncontroversial, and that strongly suggests that there is a notion of shared structure to draw on.

2. What goes for maps surely goes for models as well.

3. There are a variety of techniques, mostly statistical, for comparing graphs.

4. Fingerprints are standardly compared. Typically, what we are looking for here is congruence, but the same techniques presently

---

20. There are silly ways of defining theory accuracy that don't carry over for representational accuracy, for example, T is more accurate than T' if it contains more truths. Once you get beyond this sort of non-starter, it is pretty clear that the only way to do the trick is to say something about the similarity among the situations in which the theories are satisfied.

on offer would work for a variety of cases in which one print is a more or less distorted transformation of the other.
5. What was said about maps goes for pictures as well. In addition, pictures can be compared by a combination of transformations and resolution loss (by increasing pixel size, for example).

This list could be extended indefinitely, but I suspect length won't help: either you are sympathetic or you aren't. And in any case, the examples show at most that it might not be a waste of time to seek a serious account of shared structure. To repeat, it isn't the idea of degrees of accuracy that is at issue here, but the idea that degrees of accuracy can (at least often) be understood in terms of shared structure.

Targets and Structures

According to PTR, representation is isomorphism. Since isomorphism is a relation between structures, it follows that, strictly speaking, only structures can represent or be represented. Since we have representational correctness when the content of a representation is the same as the target of its application, it follows that targets are also, strictly speaking, structures. According to PTR, then, we speak loosely when we say, for example, that a map represents Tucson.[21] Common sense recognizes this looseness by acknowledging such facts as that a topographical map and a street map of Tucson, while both maps of Tucson, nevertheless map different things. A street map abstracts away from many features of the city, including contours and altitudes, while a topographical map abstracts away from many features, including the layout of the streets. All forms of representation, except particle-for-particle duplication, are abstract in this sense: they capture certain structures and are silent about others.[22] Indeed, it is the fact that different representational schemes often differ in what structures they can represent that makes them differentially useful and, to some extent, incommensurable in content. You can describe things you cannot picture (triangularity), and you can picture things you cannot describe (the color blue).

Strictly speaking, then, targets and contents are structures; loosely speaking they are the things having those structures. It is encouraging to note that the loose talk disappears for the most part in scientific contexts. Psycholinguists, for example, are careful to distinguish phonetic from

21. PTR is not alone in this. According to Fodor's theory (1990b), only properties can be represented. Both Dretske's theory (1981) and Millikan's (1984), on the other hand, allow for the representation of individuals.
22. Even a particle-for-particle duplicate of *t* represents everything having the same particle-for-particle structure as *t*.

syntactic representations (Fodor, Bever, and Garrett, 1974) which are representations of different structural features of the same verbal input or output. And vision theorists are careful to distinguish the different structural features of the local space that are represented at different stages of visual processing (Marr, 1982).

Targets differ from contents in one important respect, however. Consider the construction of a phrase marker in a speech recognition system. The phrase marker itself—the representation procured by the current phrase-structure intender—has a phrase structure as its content. The intender has the phrase structure *of the current input* as its target. The target, then, is not just some particular phrase structure, but rather the phrase structure of some particular thing, viz. the current input of the parser. Contents, then, are simply structures; targets are structures *of* something.[23] *Which* something is typically fixed indexically: Facts internal to a functioning chess system may determine that the representational target of a certain process on a given occasion is the current board position, but facts about the world determine which position that happens to be.

Structural Representation

In a groundbreaking paper, Chris Swoyer (1991) presents a formal account of what he calls *structural representation* (SR hereafter). There are two basic ideas here. (1) Many things represent what they do in virtue of sharing structure with what they represent. (2) SRs enable *surrogative reasoning.*

> Structural representation enables us to reason directly about a representation in order to draw conclusions about the things that it represents. By examining the behavior of a scale model of an aircraft in a wind tunnel, we can draw conclusions about a newly designed wing's response to wind shear, rather than trying it out on a Boeing 747 over Denver. By using numbers to represent the lengths of physical objects, we can represent facts about the objects numerically, perform calculations of various sorts, then translate the results back into a conclusion about the original objects. In such cases, we use one sort of thing as a surrogate in our thinking about another, and so I shall call this *surrogative reasoning.* (Swoyer, 1991, p. 449)

23. I suppose it is possible to have an abstract structure *tout court* as a target. An intender could have the function of representing triangularity or Abelian rings, for example. But such examples must be pretty rare in natural cognition if they occur at all. My suspicion is that such cases are all parasitic on language which allows us to specify abstract targets for ourselves. Language-using cognitive agents who know geometry, for example, are or emulate intenders whose function it is to represent geometric structures that are linguistically specified. More of this in chapter 10.

Surrogates, as Swoyer understands them are what I called proxies above. And Swoyer sees the point in much the same way.

> Not all representations allow detailed reasoning about the things they represent; no amount of pondering the embroidery of Hester's 'A' will reveal the details of her exploits. Still, the point of much representation is to *mediate inferences* about things in the world, and this raises what might be called the *applications problem*. The question how an abstract body of theory like mathematics can apply to concrete reality is a venerable one in philosophy, but if the following account is right, it is just a special case of a more general puzzle: How can *any* representational system—from rudimentary arithmetic to a complex natural language—be successfully applied to the world? How is such representation possible? I believe that the *best explanation* why a mathematical theory applies to the concrete phenomena it does is that it has many of the same *structural features as those phenomena*. It is a central thesis of this paper that *shared structure* of precisely this sort explains the applicability of a wide range of representational systems—including many non-mathematical ones—to the things they represent. (p. 451)

Swoyer and I disagree about language. I don't think language represents at all. A complex expression has a structure, and hence represents whatever shares that structure according to PTR. But the conventional meaning of an expression has nothing to do with its representational content in this sense. Certain formal symbol systems do exploit structural properties in a way that makes them SRs, as do certain nonphonetic writing systems such as Chinese characters and hieroglyphics. The case of mathematics, emphasized by Swoyer, is interesting because it is the mathematical structure itself—for example, the numbers with the arithmetical relations on them—rather than the symbols we use to talk and write about it that does the structural representing. Although Swoyer begins with the notion of isomorphic embeddings as an account of structural representation, he needlessly (to my mind) complicates the account to account for language. As he himself notes (p. 475), the result of abandoning PTR is to complicate and compromise the account of surrogative reasoning that largely motivates the account in the first place.

Chapter 8
Target Fixation

Understanding representational error, and hence representational explanation, requires, as we've seen, a distinction between the content of a representation and the target a tokening of a representation is aimed at. It is clear enough how to get started on the problem of what makes *t* the target of an application of *r*:

(TF)   *t* is the target of an application of *r* just in case it is the function of that tokening of *r* to represent *t*.

There is a large literature in philosophy devoted to explicating what it is for *f* to be the function of *x* in some system Σ. Since this is an essay about mental representation, a natural and attractive ploy at this point would be to point out that, however problematic the concept of function is, it *is not* a semantic concept, it *is* widely implicated in natural science that has nothing to do with mental representation, and hence it isn't my problem. Indeed, I would like to be able to say that the role of functions in target fixation simply provides one more constraint for philosophers interested in clarifying function attribution. Unfortunately, this burden shifting strategy won't do.

Functions

It *is* tempting to hope that one of the theories of functions currently on offer in the literature will complete the analysis of target fixation given in TF. But there are two rather general problems that must be solved if this is to work. The first is that available theories of functions apply to events only as instances of types: 'the function of *x* is *f*' is defined in terms of what *x* does Normally (Millikan, 1984) or typically or ideally, or what *x* does whenever some specified condition holds. But it is essential to the current project that different tokens of the type "tokenings-of-*r*" can have different representational functions, for *r* can be applied to different targets on different occasions. Not every tokening of |elm| has as its function representing elms, for, if this were the case, there could be no error.

Representational error arises when an |elm| is applied to something that isn't an elm, for example, when the function of a tokening of |elm| is to represent a beech or the number 9 or the proposition that roses are red. So we need a theory of functions that allows for the function of tokening r to differ from occasion to occasion.

The second problem that arises when we try to plug an over-the-counter analysis of functions into TF is that we need an analysis of functions that does not define correct functioning in terms of the success of some containing system or process, but allows for the fact that representational success is neither necessary nor sufficient for the nonrepresentational success of representational systems. TF will be incorrect if we expand it via a theory of functions that yields the implication that cognitive processes require representational correctness to function properly. Representational error can be quite compatible with success. Indeed, in chapter 4 I went through some pains to point out that representational inaccuracy can be a Good Thing. It is a Good Thing, for example, when a simple approximation is more tractable than a fully accurate representation. In cases of this sort, which may well be the rule rather than the exception, full accuracy may not only fail to be a necessary condition of success but be actually incompatible with it. So far as I can tell, however, every available theory of functions *does* define functions in terms of the success of some containing system or process.

So we have two problems. First, the function of tokening r on a particular occasion cannot be understood in terms of some property of the type *tokenings of r*, since different tokenings of r will often have different targets. That, of course, is precisely what creates the possibility of representational error. Second, we cannot understand "the function of this tokening of r is to represent t" in a way that implies that the successful performance of some containing system is typically or Normally contingent on r's representing t, since accurate representation is neither necessary nor sufficient for successful performance in cognitive systems.

The Theories on Offer

Theories of functions can be divided into two categories: selectionist theories and design theories. I propose to discuss each of these alternatives at a rather abstract level to see how the two problems just rehearsed arise for each of these general approaches.

Selectionist Theories
The fundamental idea of selectionist theories of functions is that the function of x is f just in case things of the type x got replicated because they

(at least sometimes) did f.[1] As it stands, this theory applies to event tokens only as instances of types. The function of *this* tokening of r is to represent t only if the function of tokening r is to represent t, for *this* tokening cannot have a selection history. As noted above, we cannot get around this by looking at the function of r-tokenings generally, for we want to allow for the fact that different tokenings of r have different targets.

There is, I think, just one way to go here: try to tie the relevant functions, hence targets, to rather specific processes or mechanisms that token r. The thought is this: whereas not every tokening of r has the same target, perhaps every tokening of r *by process P* has the same target. What is wanted, in fact, is the notion of a *t-intender*, an intender whose special business it is to represent t. Then every tokening of any representation by that intender will be aimed at (but may not hit) t. A mechanism is just the sort of thing that can have a selection history, of course, so it least makes sense to suppose that a mechanism is a t-intender, that is, has the function of producing representations of t, because it got replicated as the result of producing representations of t. An obvious difficulty with this proposal is that it requires a dedicated intender for every target the system can have, and this appears problematic to say the least. I propose to put this to one side for the moment and return to it later.

Even if we can get around this problem of needing a special intender for every target, selectionist theories run afoul of our second problem, for they define functions in terms of the success or failure of a containing system or process. To see this, note that selectionist theories assume that something must actually perform its function successfully in order to contribute to its replication. Whatever you may think of this assumption in other contexts, it won't do in the current one, for it amounts to the assumption that something is a t-intender only if it sometimes successfully represents t, and that is just the assumption we must avoid for the very good reason that it is not true. Millikan (1984) has taught us that something need not perform its Proper Function very often to get selected; we need now to note that, at least in the case of representational functions, something may be selected because of what it does, even though it *never* performs its Proper Function properly. It may be the (or a) function of the visual system, for example, to represent the spatial layout even if it never does (or did) this accurately.

It is tempting to respond to this by thinking that I must be misdescribing representational functions. Couldn't it be the function of tokening r to

---

1. In Millikan's official formulation (1984), it is the performance of the "consumers" of an intender's representational outputs that figures in the definition of proper functioning, but this makes no difference to the present point. Consumers, like intenders, will not be selected for if they are too nice about accuracy.

more or less accurately represent t, or to represent t accurately enough? But this suggestion really misses the point. The problem is that the success of the containing system cannot be assumed to be proportional to the accuracy of representation. Given the computational and external environment, there typically will be some tradeoff between tractability and accuracy that is optimal in the sense that both more accuracy and less accuracy will diminish overall performance. But even this oversimplifies matters. How much accuracy is optimal will typically vary from occasion to occasion depending on such factors as how much time and memory is available. Thus, there is no saying in general how much accuracy is optimal, hence no saying in general what the semantic conditions are under which an intender will be selected. About all that can be said is that a t-intender will be selected only if it represents t accurately enough often enough, and this is utterly trivial. We've got our work cut out for us, then, if we are going to adapt selectionist theories of functions to the theory of target fixation.

Design Theories

Design theories of functions define the function of a mechanism or process in terms of its functional role, that is, in terms of its contribution to some capacity of a containing system (Cummins, 1984). Design theories thus relativize functions to capacities of containing systems: the (or a) function of x in a system Σ is f relative to a capacity C of Σ just in case Σ's capacity C analyzes (in part) into x's capacity to f.

It is obvious that design theories, like selectionist theories, assign functions to mechanisms, processes, or event types, not to event tokens, so design theories will also saddle the theory of target fixation with the assumption of an intender for every target the system can have. It is less obvious, but also true, that design theories define functions in terms of the success of a containing system. To see this, note that an analysis of Σ's capacity C is an analysis of Σ's capacity to successfully manifest C. But we cannot, in general, assume that analysis of Σ's capacity C will turn up some intender's capacity to accurately represent t; more typically, it will analyze into some intender's capacity to represent t accurately enough (but not too accurately) on enough occasions. This is just the problem we encountered in connection with selectionist theories.

The Problem of Valuable Inaccuracy

What we have to deal with are situations in which a t-intender typically or always produces a representation r that is, in some respects, and in some degree, an inaccurate representation of t but still "good enough."

Our problem is this: how can it be the function, or a function, of a mechanism to represent t if neither it nor its ancestors have actually succeeded in accurately representing t?

The key to understanding this issue is to realize that it is the (or a) function of N to produce representations of t if it is the representational relation—the degree of fit—between t and the tokens N produces that underlies N's contribution to the system that contains it. To get a feel for this, we may imagine the situation in which a map M is completely accurate for $m1$, but used by Σ to get around the somewhat different $m2$. To understand Σ's success and failures in negotiating $m2$, and M's contributions to these, we have to know how accurately M represents $m2$, since Σ's errors are measured relative to $m2$, M's target on the occasions in question. Hence, Σ's capacity to negotiate $m2$ as well as it does cannot be understood in terms of its capacity to perfectly represent $m1$, even though any representation that represents $m1$ perfectly will in fact represent $m2$ accurately enough (and in just the right way) to explain Σ's performance in $m2$. For while it is true and lawlike that Σ performs as it does in $m2$ because it perfectly represents $m1$, this holds only because of the relation between $m1$ and $m2$. To assess Σ's performance in $m2$, we need somehow to assess Σ's representation of $m2$. We can do this by assessing Σ's representation of $m1$, but only if we are already in a position to assess how well $m1$ represents $m2$. Since M and $m1$ are isomorphic by hypothesis, assessing the representational relation between $m1$ and $m2$ is equivalent to assessing the representational relation between M and $m2$.

Note, though, that while it is the fact that the map drives Σ's behavior in $m2$ that makes it evident that $m2$ is the target, it isn't the fact that the map drives Σ's behavior in $m2$ that *makes* $m2$ the map's target as a matter of constitutive definition. We don't have here an example that can be generalized into a kind of output-transduction definition of targeting, for, in general, there need be no such direct relation as is imagined in this case. R may not be used by Σ to behave in t at all, or only in ways that are mediated by lots of other stuff. I can use a map to represent China without leaving Tucson. Still, the illustration points us in the right direction, for it is surely the fact that successes and failures of various cognitive tasks have to be assessed in the light of how well the map represents China, rather than somewhere else, that constitutes the fact that the target of the map is China.

Selectionist theories can handle inaccuracy by requiring that the (or a) function of N is to produce representations of t if, historically, it was N's capacity, or the capacity of its ancestors, to produce representations that, to some degree, were accurate representations of t that accounts for the replication of N. This formulation makes room for the possibility that neither N nor its ancestors ever produced fully accurate representations of t.

So long as it is the relative accuracy of N's productions vis à vis t, rather than something else, that matters to N's selection history, selectionist theories will pick out t as the target of the representations N produces.

An exactly similar move will allow design theories to accommodate inaccuracy. So long as it is the capacity of N to produce representations, however good or bad, of t rather than something else that is involved in a proper functional analysis of a capacity of a system containing N, design theories will count N as a t-intender relative to the analyzed capacity of the containing system.

Intenders

Both selectionist and design theories of functions imply that individual events such as a particular tokening of a representation have functions only as instances of a type. Since different tokenings of the same representation can have different functions, we cannot define "t is the target of this tokening of r" in terms of the function of r tokenings generally. Rather, we have been forced to suppose that for each target t that Σ can have, Σ must incorporate a mechanism—a t-intender—whose special business it is to produce representations of t. We may then define target fixation in terms of the functions of such mechanisms:

> (TF) the target of a particular tokening of r is t just in case that tokening of r is produced by a mechanism N, and it is the (or a) function of N to produce representations of t.

This formulation of TF is problematic, as noted briefly above, because it requires a system to incorporate an intender for every target it can have. It seems pretty obvious, however, that humans, at any rate, can have an unbounded number of targets. Since an unbounded number of intenders is a lot to swallow, it would seem to follow that TF is hopeless.

Fortunately, things are not as bad as they seem. There are two factors that make an unbounded set of targets possible. The first is that a system's contribution to target fixation is typically indexical in character; the second is that intenders can be "nested" in a way that gives rise to a familiar kind of combinatorics. Let's look at these two factors in turn.

Indexicality

Recall the chess example: on a particular occasion, Σ's target in producing a representation r will be a certain board position, say P3. This target gets fixed jointly by two factors: (1) the fact that the intender that produced r has as its function the production of a representation of the current position, and (2) the fact that the current position on the occasion in question was P3. Indexical intenders of this sort are common in biological and artificial systems. Typical targets of this kind include the following: the current local spatial layout, the phonetic (syntactic) structure of the current verbal input, the object of current foveation, the current hypothesis, the conclusion of current interest, the spatial layout at p, the syntactic structure of the current verbal output, the name of the person just introduced, the last letter presented, and so on. The indexicality of intenders has the consequence that a system can have an unbounded number of targets even though it has a finite number of intenders. The current phrase-structure intender in a parser, for example, accounts for as many targets as there are phrase structures.[2]

A little reflection suggests that intenders in finite but plastic systems must be indexical in this way. Sensory systems must be able to generate representations of *current stimuli.* A sensory system that was rigid, that is, aimed at a determinate target, might be fast and reliable, but would have limited usefulness. Analogously, reasoning systems must contain procedures that apply to the current premise set whatever that might happen to be. A reasoning procedure that applied to only one particular premise set would hardly count as a reasoning procedure at all.

Nested Intenders
This book begins by considering an intender whose target is the position after M, where M is some finite sequence of chess moves. Evidently this intender—call it $pa(M)$—cannot do its stuff unless M is bound to some representation of a move sequence. That representation is in turn produced by another intender—call it m—whose business it is to produce representations of move sequences. We may think of $pa(M)$ as a function of M, but we may also think of the intender m as nested in (or called by) the intender $pa(M)$, which has as many targets as there are sequence representations in m's repertoire. The intender m itself, presumably, generates representations of move sequences from representations of moves. If a move is represented as an ordered pair of board positions, then move representations are in turn generated from position representations. Underlying the production of a representation of the position after M, then, are a number of intenders nested (interacting) in a way that is the familiar bread and butter of computer programming.

2. Note that a finite parser, that is, a parser with finite resources, will not, in fact, be able to represent every phrase structure, hence will be capable of targets it cannot hit. Targeting a phrase structure that is too large to represent will result in representational error (assuming a representation is generated), but not necessarily forced error. The system may well have a representational system that is capable of representing a phrase structure of any size, but be unable to exploit this system fully because of memory or time limitations. Such cases need to be distinguished from genuine cases of forced error in which no representation exists in the system's representational scheme that hits the target.

Taken individually or together, nesting and the indexicality of intenders allows a bounded system to intend targets drawn from an unbounded set. We need not worry, then, that both selectionist and design theories of functions will, in combination with TF, imply an intender for every target. The required intenders are on the cards in any case, even in rather simple artificial systems.

Targets and Teleology

Lots of theories of content appeal to functions in one way or another. Milllikan's (1984) theory takes the content of a representation to be fixed by the Proper Functions of its producers/consumers. Dretske's (1981) theory takes content to be fixed by functions to indicate. Fodor once proposed a theory (1990a) that, in effect, fixes content by appeal to the functions of property-detection systems. All of these theories have been subjected to crippling critiques. We are now in a position to see, however, that teleology does have a proper place in the theory of mental representation, viz. in the theory of intentionality or target fixation. It is tempting to speculate, indeed, that it has been largely intuitions about target fixation that have driven teleological theories of content. In chapter 9, we uncover some further evidence for this idea when we find that it is a failure to distinguish targets and contents that fuels Twin Earth–style arguments for anti-individualism and "wide content."

Thought and Targets

Thought, conscious thought, appears to present the following problem for PTR:

> 1. When I think of Anna Moffo, I am not *thereby* thinking of a numerical structure.
> 2. Yet according to PTR, the representation I token represents a numerical structure if it represents anything.

How are these to be reconciled?

One could give up number 1: I *am* thinking of a numerical structure, I just don't realize it. But this is a dead end, for we still have a difference between thought and representation: I think I'm thinking of Anna Moffo, but I don't think I'm thinking of a numerical structure. But any reason for supposing that thoughts about opera stars are also thoughts about numbers is going to be a reason for supposing that thoughts about thoughts are thoughts about numbers.

One could give up number 2. Representation is, or can be, exactly as nice (i.e., discriminating) as thought. This is what everyone supposes, and the result is an endless and hopeless pursuit of a theory of representation that makes representation exactly as nice as thought.

A third possibility has been overlooked: when I think of Anna Moffo, I represent a person and a number (among other things). But if Anna Moffo is the target of my application of the relevant representation, and the number isn't, then what will make the difference between error and correctness will be the relation between my representation and Anna Moffo. The relation between my representation and the numbers will be irrelevant. Hence the sense that the representation is pointed at Anna Moffo and not at a number. It is targets that are nice, not contents.

Can I think about Anna Moffo when my representational target is the number 9? I ask myself how many planets there are in our solar system, and what comes to mind is an image of Anna Moffo. But is this really aiming an image of Anna Moffo at the number of planets? Probably not. A more plausible story is that I have learned a special convention encoding numbers as the names of opera stars. As it happens, "Anna Moffo" isn't covered by this convention, though I have forgotten this, or never knew. Asked after the number of planets, I aim a representation of Anna Moffo at the number of planets. This is error: I've represented Anna Moffo in a case in which the target is the number 9. But this doesn't even seem like thinking of Anna Moffo. The moral of the story is that what we take ourselves to be thinking about are the targets of our representations, not their contents.

There is a temptation to identify the contents of one's representations with what one takes them (knows them) to be about. But when I harbor a representation whose content is Anna Moffo, but whose target is Renata Tebaldi, who do I suppose myself to be thinking about? Tebaldi. I imagine a face, say, trying to picture Tebaldi in my mind. I think I have succeeded, but, in fact, I have imagined A.M.'s face. In a case like this, there are two things available to introspection: the image and what it is for. The target is transparent to introspection here: it is Tebaldi, and that is who I take myself to be thinking about. And the image is transparent to introspection as well, of course. What is not transparent to introspection, however, is who the image actually represents, though this *would* be transparent (though not to introspection alone) if Moffo and Tebaldi stood before me and identified themselves. To repeat: one's sense that one is thinking of Tebaldi and not Moffo or the number 9 is not a sense about the contents of one's thoughts but about their targets.

Chapter 9
Why There Is No Symbol Grounding Problem

Some Representations Are Not Symbols

We need to begin with a point about the scope of the problem. The problem about grounding is not just a problem about symbols; it is supposed to be a problem about representations generally. It is just that the problem became popular when symbols were the only representations in the running in cognitive science. So the problem, if there is one, is the representation grounding problem. Nevertheless, we should keep in mind that the discussion in the literature (Harnad, 1990; Fodor, 1990b) may be misleading in some respects because it has been conducted exclusively with symbolic representational schemes in mind. It should not surprise us greatly if it turns out that symbols are a rather special case.

What is the Representation Grounding Problem?

There are two ways of seeing how the grounding problem arises.

1. *Wide content.* Nearly every philosopher writing about mental representation these days believes something like this: Suppose I harbor a |water|, that is, a mental representation meaning water. Since, on Earth, water is H_2O, and I'm on Earth, my |water|s refer to H_2O. My duplicate on Twin Earth harbors |water|s too, since he is a duplicate. However, since the counterpart of water on Twin Earth is in fact XYZ, not H_2O, my twin's |water|s mean XYZ. Because my twin and I are duplicates, this difference in the content of our representations cannot arise from any internal differences between us. What, then, makes his |water|s mean XYZ and mine mean H_2O? The schematic answer is: his |water|s are *grounded in* XYZ, whereas mine are *grounded in* H_2O. Of course, this is not a solution. We have just given the solution a name. The problem is to say what grounding is.

2. *Multiple interpretability.* Imagine a chess system. It takes as input a representation of a board position, and gives a representation of a board position as output, the output representing a position that

differs from the position represented by the input by one legal move. What makes this a chess system is the fact that its inputs and outputs are interpreted as chess positions. But anything that is interpretable as a chess system is also interpretable in many other ways. For example, any systematic way of numbering the possible board positions will yield an interpretation of the system as computing a numerical function. When I play chess, however, I am playing chess, not computing a numerical function. What, then, makes my representations representations of chess positions rather than representations of numbers? The schematic answer is: my representations are *grounded in* chess positions, not numbers. Of course, this isn't a solution. We have just given the solution a name. The problem is to say what grounding is.

Meaning and Grounding

On the face of it, there appear to be two problems that any naturalistic theory of mental representation must solve.

1. The problem of meaningfulness: What makes a physical something a representation? Here the question is what makes mere form (or whatever) into meaning.

2. The problem of meaning assignment: What gives a representation the particular satisfaction condition it has? Here the problem is to formulate a theory that will assign the right meanings to the elements of a scheme of representation.

Once we notice the grounding problem, though, the problem of meaningfulness and the problem of meaning assignment seem to be the same problem at bottom. For a representation to have a "real" meaning ("underived intentionality") is for it to be hooked up to the world, for example, to H_2O, in the way we call *meaning H_2O*. So, if you could figure out what hooks |water| to H_2O on Earth and to XYZ on Twin Earth (or hooks |P-K4|s to chess moves), you would have figured out what attaches representations to meanings, hence figured out what makes mere form into meaning.

There has to be something wrong with this idea, however, because it is pretty clear on reflection that the sorts of grounding relations that have been proposed in the literature are neither necessary nor sufficient for representational accuracy, and hence cannot be necessary or sufficient for representational content either.

Here is a Twin Earth fable. There are two identical mazes, $m1$ and $m2$. I make a map M of $m1$ by taking an aerial photo. I use this map to get through $m1$, something I must do to get food. WW-III occurs, wiping out airplanes and the like. The map is carefully copied by successive generations, etc. (The point is to hook me and my use of the map to $m1$ in whatever way might be thought essential to grounding the map in $m1$. Insert your favorite story.)

Now: Is M an accurate representation of $m2$?

Of course.

First, nothing could be better than M for $m2$: If you want to get around $m2$, you certainly wouldn't want to trade M for something else, for example, for a properly grounded map. So grounding isn't *necessary* for representing accurately.

Second, grounding isn't sufficient for accurate representation. Suppose there is an "error" in M, so that it isn't quite accurate for $m1$, the maze in which it is "grounded." And suppose that $m2$ differs slightly from $m1$ so that the map is a perfect map for $m2$. Surely M represents $m2$, not $m1$. Or rather, M is a more accurate representation of $m2$ than of $m1$.

Given these two points, it is evident that *accuracy* is independent of "grounding," that is, independent of any facts about the user of the representation, and how that user is "embedded" in the environment.

One might object that M *is* grounded in $m2$, the grounding consisting in the very fact that the system using it is *in* $m2$, using M to mediate its navigation of $m2$. But it is no part of the case I have imagined that M is actually used to negotiate $m2$. The case depends rather on the obvious fact that M's accuracy vis à vis $m2$ can be evaluated independently of its use or its origins.

I have encountered two kinds of complaint about this argument. The first is that symbols may well need grounding even though maps don't. The second complaint is a standard conventionalist complaint: it is that maps cannot really be evaluated for accuracy independently of their uses or origins. Let us look at these complaints in turn.

I propose to concede the first complaint. Primitive symbols have no intrinsic representational content, hence can be tied to their meanings only by some "third man." Typically, this is a convention of use. Perhaps there are nonconventional ways to tie primitive symbols to their meanings, as causal theorists and adaptational role theorists think. But whether the factor that relates primitive symbols to their meanings is conventional or not, it is certainly not intrinsic to the symbol in the way that what makes a map a map of x and not y *is* intrinsic to the map. So primitive symbols have to be "grounded." So much the worse for symbolic theories of mental representation. Symbols are good communicative vehicles, but bad representational vehicles.

The second complaint—that maps are just as conventional as symbols—is more serious. That there are representational schemes whose elements are "intrinsically meaningful" is the burden of chapter 7, which will have to stand on its merits as my response to the conventionalist complaint. It is worth remembering the Autobots, however: they are guided by maps whose relation to the terrain is surely independent of what anyone thinks, hence independent of convention by any standard of convention that has ever been proposed (e.g., Lewis, 1969).

Deconstructing Twin Earth Arguments

If grounding is irrelevant to content, how is it that the Twin Earth cases make it seem that "context" or "grounding" *is* essential to content? Thinking back on the Twin Earth cases, it seems clear that the issue is not, as it were, what information there is about H_2O or XYZ in a |water|, but rather which stuff my |water|s are "aimed at." This suggests that the Twin Earth cases, if they show anything, show that the *target* of my uses of |water| is H_2O rather than XYZ. Not of all of my uses, of course, but of those uses Fodor (1990b) would call my labeling uses.

"What's that stuff you're drinking?," you ask.

"Water," I respond.

Here, it seems, the target of my utterance of 'water' is H_2O, not XYZ, for what is wanted is a representation of what I'm drinking, and I'm drinking H_2O. It is plausible to suppose that a comparable use of |water| would have H_2O as its target as well. On the assumption that my |water|s are satisfied by H_2O, we have a case of correct use. So far, so good. Maybe wide content intuitions are just misplaced intuitions about targets.

Unfortunately, this diagnosis is just too neat to be true. Part of the Twin Earth story is that I can't tell H_2O from XYZ, and this makes it plausible to suppose that my |water|s are as accurate when applied to XYZ as they are when applied to H_2O.[1] This, however, will entail that my uses of |water| on Twin Earth will also be correct, provided only that the target of my |water|s is XYZ on Twin Earth. But what else could their targets be? This is supposed to be a labeling use, and the target of a labeling use is surely the stuff labeled—XYZ in this case. So: If we individuate

---

1. I think this is not just plausible, but close to inevitable. For suppose my |water|s are accurate representations of H_2O but not of XYZ. Then I have the *representational* means to distinguish H_2O from XYZ. How will we square this with the assumption that I cannot tell them apart? We shall have to suppose the problem is epistemic, a case of unforced error. But, surely, if I have the representational resources, I will be in a position to appreciate evidence and arguments presented by experts, or at least to learn to appreciate them.

None of this detail is ever supplied in Twin Earth discussions because no one supposes it necessary. Why not? Because everyone is supposing that there is nothing *in the representation itself* to distinguish H_2O from XYZ. But from that it simply follows that applications of |water| to either will be equally accurate. And, of course, on the assumption that |water| is a primitive symbol, there is nothing in the representation itself to distinguish H_2O from XYZ.

targets widely, making the target in either case the stuff I am drinking, then my labeling uses of |water| will be correct in response to either H_2O or XYZ. How, then, does everyone get the result that my labeling uses of |water| are errors on Twin Earth?[2]

The disappointing answer is: confusion of targets and contents. Here's how it works.

1. I said "water" (I used a |water|) to label what is in fact H_2O. H_2O, then, was my target.
2. The target, H_2O, is what I meant by my utterance of "water" (my use of |water|).
3. H_2O, then, is what I referred to.
4. My uses of "water" (|water|) refer to H_2O.
5. So, when I use "water" (|water|) on Twin Earth to label XYZ, I make an error, for what I mean is H_2O.

As this progression makes clear, expressions like "what I referred to," "what I meant," and the like are ambiguous. Sometimes they mean targets, sometimes contents. You say, "I used M and got around the city with no problem." "Which city do you mean?" ("Which city are you referring to?"), I ask. Here, I am asking for your target, the city against which M's accuracy is to be measured. "Here is the map of the city I was telling you about," you say. "Which city do you mean?," I ask. Here, I am asking for the content, that is, for the city the map actually represents. The standard Twin Earth cases simply trade on this ambiguity in semantic terms. The potential for ambiguity derives from the fact that there are two senses in which representations are "pointed at" the world, the content sense and the target sense, but the distinction is not marked in ordinary vocabulary. The distinction is *there*, as the example just rehearsed makes clear, but it is marked only by different uses of the same expressions in ordinary language. Once we introduce a technical vocabulary for the distinction— 'content' and 'target'—the thinking behind the Twin Earth argument no longer has a plausible expression. Those cases turn crucially on sliding from the sense of "what 'water' refers to," which means *target*, to the sense in which it means *content*. You begin with an indexical target identification—the kind of stuff I'm now drinking—take this to be *what I referred to*, and hence to be a specification of content.

Note, by the way, that I might very well need, on occasion, a representation that is satisfied by H_2O and not XYZ. If |water| is the only tool in the box, I will label the stuff I'm drinking |water|, and this will be an

<hr>

2. We can, of course, imagine uses of |water| that have XYZ as their target, not H_2O:

"What was that stuff you drank at the going away party on Twin Earth?," you ask. "Water," I reply.

error—a forced error—in cases in which the target is H_2O *specifically. A* use of |water| in such a case would be like a case of responding to a cat with |animal| when what I need is a representation of *cats*. This suggests a related but slightly different diagnosis of the Twin Earth argument that turns on an ambiguity in the target rather than an ambiguity in semantic terms. You begin with an indexical identification of the target of a use of |water|: The stuff I'm drinking, viz. H_2O. You assume that this is a correct use. Since the content of a representation is just its target in cases of correct use, it follows that the content of |water| is H_2O. Hence, |water| does not apply correctly to XYZ. The problem here is that we have not been given enough information about the target to determine whether we have a case of correct use or not. If the target is H_2O specifically, then we do not have a case of correct use but a case of forced (but nonserious) error,[3] hence no case for saying the content is H_2O. If the target is some less specific kind of stuff, a kind of stuff that includes XYZ, then we arguably have a case of correct use, but we still have no case for saying the content is H_2O.

Modestly careful attention to the target-content distinction undermines Twin Earth arguments for the conclusion that mental representations get their contents by being "grounded" in extrapsychological circumstances. Still, there is something to the idea that intuitions about the need to "ground" mental representations in the extrapsychological are really legitimate intuitions about target fixation. Unlike contents, targets are not independent of "grounding," if by grounding we mean some nonindividualistic property of the representing system. This is because we often need an individuating representation of *that kind of stuff*, or of *that thing*. In these situations, targets are fixed, in part at least, by a nonsemantic relation to the thing itself, for example, by the fact that I am touching it with my index finger, or drinking it. Targets aren't always fixed like this, but they typically are, as we saw in chapter 8, and that is enough to make the theory of target fixation a "wide" theory.

Deconstruction of Multiple Interpretability Arguments

Let μ be a numerical function isomorphic to the function on board positions computed by some chess system. What makes a chess system a chess system rather than a system that calculates μ? We are now in a position to see that this question is ambiguous. In one sense, a system is a

3. We are assuming, remember, that I don't have the representational resources to distinguish H_2O from XYZ. Hence, I have no representation that will hit the target H_2O specifically, though, of course, I have various representations that will be satisfied by some such target as *the kind of stuff I am drinking*, for example, |inorganic liquid| or |water|.

chess system if the targets of its representations are chess positions, that is, if it is chess positions that are *intended* by the applications of its representations. A system is a chess system in this sense—in intention—*regardless* of the contents of its representations, and hence regardless of whether it succeeds in playing chess at all. So, if we ask what makes a system a chess system rather than a μ-system, the answer, in one sense of the question, is: whatever fixes targets. Target fixation is the topic of chapter 8. There we saw that targets are fixed in part by the world. The target of a specific application of R might be the current position. This much is determined by factors internal to the system. But it is the world that determines which position the current position is, and hence whether R is error or not. In this sense, intentional contents, that is, targets, might properly be said to be "grounded in" a relation the system bears to the world it is operating in.

In another sense, a system is a chess system rather than a μ-computer if its representations have chess positions rather than numbers as contents. And that, according to the Picture Theory of Representation (PTR), the theory of chapter 7, has to do with the structure of the representations: Content is determined by the structure of a system's representations, not by any causal or historical or social relation the system bears to the world. Of course, PTR, as we've seen, entails a kind of multiple interpretability. If a solution to the grounding problem requires explaining what makes a map of Tucson not a map of Twin Tucson, where it is understood that this is not a question about targets, then the grounding problem has no solution. We do need to explain why thinking about Tucson isn't thinking about Twin Tucson, but this isn't a matter of representational contents, it is a matter of targets.

Meaningfulness and Grounding

A common response to Searle's famous Chinese Room argument (1980) is to suppose that what makes the Chinese characters meaningless to the Chinese Room is that they are not "grounded" in anything. What appears "from the outside" to be conversation, or rather correspondence, appears "from the inside" to be a complex game of trading meaningless characters. The characters I trade with the outside would seem meaningful to me, the story goes, if they were "grounded" for me in the objects, states of affairs, etc., that they conventionally represent to speakers of Chinese. In correspondence I use what, unbeknown to me, is the character for *house*, but I never connect that character with houses. If a character is to mean *house*, it had better be connected to houses somehow.

There is, of course, a kernel of truth in this: being able to use a word or character in conversation or correspondence is not sufficient for knowing what it means. A program, therefore, whose execution enabled me to use Chinese characters in correspondence would not necessarily be a program whose execution would make me an understander of Chinese. Admirable as this point is, however, it is not, as it stands, focused on the problem at hand, for our mental representations are not used in conversation or correspondence. They are not used by me at all, in the sense in which I use the words of a language I understand. Still, the point does strongly suggest to many that a necessary condition for making something meaningful is to "ground" it somehow in the objects that satisfy it. Grounding, in this sense, is a matter of there being a cognitive connection of some kind between the representation and what it represents.

I think the felt need for this sort of "grounding" derives largely from concentrating on *symbolic* representation. Primitive symbols are arbitrary, and this means, as we have seen, that they can have no intrinsic representational content. Thus, for symbols, being meaningful just reduces to being understood, and, as reflection on the Chinese Room makes clear, *understanding* a symbol (or any kind of representation) requires relating it to something else. Symbols don't mean, in other words, except to the extent that they mean*for*. But for nonsymbolic representations like maps, being meaningful does not reduce to, or even require, being understood or having a meaning*for*.[4] Maps represent whether or not anyone does or can understand them. As the argument in Meaning and Grounding (above) shows, the content of a map is independent of its "grounding." Once we see this, we see that grounding is not generally required for meaningfulness, though it is required (always?) for meaning*for*ness. The question therefore arises as to why it *is* necessary for the meaningfulness of a symbol. And once we see symbols as the rather special case they are, the answer is not far to seek: for a symbol to be meaningful is for it to be understood, and understanding requires grounding. Grounding is therefore not an issue for representation, but for understanding, and relates to meaningfulness only because symbolic meaningfulness requires understanding, that is, because symbolic meaning is based on meaning*for*, and is therefore not really a *semantic* matter at all, but a cognitive one. Grounding of the sort the Chinese Room argument invites us to consider is therefore not a prerequisite of meaning, but a consequence of it: it is just the sort of cognitive relation that we are supposed to explain by appeal to representation and computation.

---

4. Remember: meaning*for* is a cognitive relation, hence not a candidate for explaining cognition. Anyone who argues for the reduction of meaning to meaning*for* is arguing that meaning (or representation) cannot possibly explain cognition. That might be right, of course, but it is beside the present inquiry, which is to determine whether it is possible to formulate a viable theory of content that is consistent with current cognitive theory.

Chapter 10
Language and Communication

Some things that are characterized semantically—mental representations, the weights in a connectionist network—are in the representation business. Other things that are characterized semantically—the expressions of a language and people's uses of them—are in the communication business. And still other semantically characterized things—maps, graphs, pictures—are in both the representation and the communication business: they are used to communicate what they represent.

We have a perfectly good word for the things that are in the representation business: "representations." We do not, however, have a word for the things in the communication business. *Communications* are the things communicated, not the communicative vehicles. *Communicators* are the agents that utter the vehicles, not the vehicles themselves. What I need is a word for the communicative vehicles themselves, words, for example, and since we do not have one, I am in the position of having to either invent one or give a special sense to a word already in use. I tried "expressions" for a while, but this is a word deeply entrenched in mathematics where it applies to the elements of a formalism that might be in the representation business. With some trepidation, I have settled on "signals." I will say that representations *have* meanings, that is, that they represent their contents, and that signals *convey* messages, that is, that they communicate something to someone.[1]

The distinction I have in mind here is like the old distinction between eminent and formal reality. A popular theory of representation and perception a few centuries back, Aristotelian in inspiration, went like this. Things are a combination of form and matter. A physical triangle or dog is physical matter informed by *triangularity* or *doghood*. An idea of triangularity or doghood is mental matter informed by *triangularity* or *doghood*. So one can have triangularity or doghood in two different kinds of media,

---

1. Since 'convey' and 'communicate' are success verbs, strictly speaking, we should say that the function of a signal is to convey/communicate a message. I will ignore this nicety.

physical matter or mental matter. To mentally represent triangularity is to have your mind stuff informed by the very same form that makes something physical triangular. When you see a triangular thing, there is a transfer of form from the thing to the mind, in something like the way that pressing a triangular object into a block of wax is a transfer of form. When I say "triangle" to you, the form in my idea has to be carried to your mind by my word. The word, however, is not informed by *triangularity*, for while one can have a triangle in physical matter, and a triangle in idea, one cannot have triangular sound. So, *triangularity* does not inform the word, but it is still in it eminently, *conveyed* by it in such a way that your mind, on the receiving end, can reconstitute the form in your mind stuff. It works like the *Star Trek* transporter. When Captain Kirk is transported from the *Enterprise* to the surface, his form is conveyed, but not possessed, by the signal that travels from ship to surface.

The central thesis of this chapter is that natural languages are conventional signaling schemes, not representational schemes. Natural languages are in the communication business, not the representation business. Words, I maintain, convey concepts. They don't have representational contents at all; they don't mean, they only mean*for*. To get a grip on this thesis, we need first to understand concepts and their role in communication.

Concepts

Concepts can be understood in either of two ways:

> 1. Concepts can be understood as abstract objects that stand to terms as sentences stand to propositions, that is, as constituents of propositions. that is, Thought of this way, concepts are not supposed to be psychological items at all, but semantic values on a par with propositions. Plato's Forms are concepts in this sense, I suppose.
> 2. Concepts can be understood as psychological items. There are two variations on this usage that need to be distinguished:
> a. Concepts are elements of a scheme of mental representation. Thus, Fodor sometimes writes as if having the concept CAT is the same as having a |cat|.
> b. Concepts are knowledge structures, that is, structures of attitudes. This seems to be the predominant usage in psychology. In this sense, to have an innate concept of an object, for example, is to have innate knowledge of what it is to be an object.[2]

2. "Knowledge," as used in psychology, implies neither truth nor justification. A bit of knowledge, in this sense, is an attitude, perhaps unconscious, that is treated by the cognitive system as if it were knowledge in the philosopher's sense.

There is no substantive issue as to whether concepts are "really" abstract objects or psychological items; it is just a matter of choice as to how one uses the word. I plan to use it in the psychological sense.

There *is* a substantive dispute underlying the distinction between (2a) and (2b), however. This is because concepts are alleged to have certain psychological functions. Concepts are typically invoked as:

i. Word meanings
ii. The mental structures that mediate recognition of the objects that fall under them
iii. The mental structures that mediate reasoning about the objects that fall under them
iv. Constituents of thoughts about the objects that fall under them.[3]

Once we see the distinction between representations and attitudes, we see that there is a substantive issue concerning whether representations or attitudes do or could have any or all of these functions. To keep (2a) and (2b) distinct, therefore, I'll write 'CAT' for the concept of a cat, and (as always) I'll write '|cat|' for the mental representation of the property of being a cat. Using this notation, the dispute is over whether, for example, CATs are |cat|s.

I will follow current psychological theory (Smith and Medin, 1981) and assume that concepts are knowledge structures as in (2b) above.[4] We'll see shortly that this view has some advantages over the view that concepts are representations. As we saw in chapter 7, the majority view has it that my ELEVATOR is a knowledge structure, not an |elevator|. It is, to a first approximation, everything I know about elevators, organized in a way that allows selective retrieval of various chunks depending on such things as what other concepts happen to be active and what retrieval cues are in the offing.

The idea that concepts are complex knowledge structures has a number of important consequences.

1. Although concepts are identified semantically via what they are concepts *of* (e.g., the concept *of an elevator*) their semantic IDs are not their representational contents. My knowledge of elevators is not a representation of the property of being an elevator. A knowledge structure has a satisfaction condition, of course—a truth condition, actually—but that is quite distinct from its semantic ID. If my knowledge of ferrets consists of

---

3. Role iv, we will see shortly, is a confusion based on the Language of Thought hypothesis together with the idea that concepts are representations.
4. Most of the psychological literature, like most of the philosophical literature, doesn't distinguish attitudes and representations—with the consequence that complex knowledge structures are called representations.

their being furry minklike mammals that are used for hunting rabbits and are the subjects of some surprising (and brutal) experiments having to do with cortical plasticity (Sur, Garraghty, and Roe, 1988; Pallas, Roe, and Sur, 1990; Sur, Pallas, and Roe, 1990), then ferrets have to be furry mink-like mammals used for hunting mammals and featured in plasticity experi-ments if my knowledge is to be true. But my FERRET is simply a concept *of ferrets*. I think it is the practice of identifying concepts semantically that encourages the mistaken idea that concepts are representations. But iden-tifying something by specifying what it is about is not the same as speci-fying its representational content. There are books about elevators, but these are not representations of elevators. The concept of an elevator is like a book about elevators. It is a lot of organized knowledge *about ele-vators*, so we call it a concept of an elevator. But an ELEVATOR no more has the class of elevators as extension then a book about elevators does. It isn't the right sort of thing to have an extension.

2. My knowledge of elevators differs from yours in various ways: it may be more or less *complete*, it may be more or less *accurate*, and it may be organized differently. In spite of this, my knowledge and your knowl-edge of elevators both count as ELEVATORS because they are both organized knowledge structures with a characteristic cognitive function—that's what makes them concepts—and they are both structured knowl-edge *of elevators*—that is what makes them ELEVATORS rather than CATS.

3. Which parts or aspects of one's knowledge of elevators happen to be activated or accessible at a given time will depend on a number of fac-tors, including how one's knowledge is organized, what cues are oper-ative, and the state of activation of one's other concepts. Thus, the "same concept" as individuated semantically may have quite different properties on different occasions.

4. Acquiring a concept is a matter of acquiring the relevant knowledge and organizing it. It follows from this that one must have or acquire knowledge of Xs before one can have the concept of an X. It also follows that concepts might be partly innate, and partly acquired, as, for example, our concept of an object seems to be (Spelke, 1990).[5]

The organization is important. Knowledge of elevators won't function as a concept unless it is unified and structured properly. How the uni-

---

5. Locke supposed that one must have the idea of a cat before one could have knowledge of cats (*Essay Concerning Human Understanding*). If Locke meant ideas to be concepts—things that underwrite object recognition, word understanding, and reasoning—then he was wrong. If he meant ideas to be representations, he might have been right to think that ideas must precede knowledge. (But even there, a qualification is required to cover the fact that one can have an attitude about Xs even though one cannot represent the property of being an X.) I think it is pretty clear from the text that Locke wanted it both ways.

fication and structuring is done in humans—indeed, how it could be done at all—is a matter of intensive research. This is what all the research on "knowledge representation"—research on frames, scripts, semantic nets, and the like—is about.

5. One is said to have *the concept of X* when one's knowledge of *Xs* is adequate. What counts as adequacy, however, may well differ depending on the context of concept attribution, since knowledge that is accurate *enough* and complete *enough* for some purposes may not be enough for others. What counts as an adequate concept of weight in ordinary life may not count as adequate in a physics class. (This is one of the reasons psychologists studying concept acquisition generally "operationalize," that is, specify an explicit experimental criterion that has to be met if a subject is to count as having a given concept). It can therefore happen that one can have a concept of elevators—an organized structure of knowledge about elevators—yet not count, for the purposes at hand, as having the concept of an elevator.

6. Concepts are not, in general, constituents of attitudes. It is attitudes, rather, that make up concepts. It follows that it is possible in principle to have the belief that, for example, the currently foveated object is a mouse without having the concept of a mouse. All that is required is a currently-foveated-object intender and a |mouse|. This would be an inexpressible belief, since we are supposing that one does have to have a MOUSE to understand the sentence, 'The currently foveated object is a mouse'.

So much for concepts. Much more could be said, but this is enough to ground the following discussion.

Communication and Language[6]

The received view about linguistic communication is this: Source (the communicator) encodes a thought that *p* in a sentence of *L* that expresses the proposition that *p*, and receiver (the communicatee) decodes the sentence into a thought that *p*. For this to work, both source and receiver have to know the meanings of the sentences of *L*. Since there are an unbounded number of sentences with distinct meanings, users of *L* must be able to compute the meaning of a sentence given its syntax and the meanings of its terms. On one popular version of this story, a logical form is recovered from the surface structure, and then a truth condition is computed from the satisfaction conditions of the terms using standard

6. The inspiration for much of the next two sections comes from Bennett (1973, 1976), which in turn draws heavily from Grice (1957, 1975) and Lewis (1969). See Cummins (1979) for a more extensive discussion of this material.

Tarskian semantics. The terms, together with their satisfaction conditions, are simply stored in a mental lexicon which is large but finite.

On my view of things, the terms of a language are signals, not representations, and therefore don't have satisfaction conditions. So I cannot tell the standard story. I can't tell any story that involves the idea that using a language requires knowing the semantic properties of its expressions, because, on my view, linguistic expressions don't have semantic properties. They have meaningsfor, but not meanings.

There is an alternative to the idea that using a language requires knowing what its terms mean. Read Grice (1957) on non-natural meaning as an analysis of meaningfor and we get a story about communication that is consistent with the idea that linguistic expressions are signals, not representations. I'm going to take some time to spell out this alternative in enough detail to lend color to the idea that communication generally, and linguistic communication in particular, can be understood without supposing that communicative vehicles—words, gestures, etc.—must have semantic properties. Here, then, is a Grician analysis of meaningfor.

> (GC)   If S (source) issues (utters, gestures, writes, etc.) e intending thereby to get R (receiver) to think that P, and relies for the achievement of this upon the Grician Mechanism (GM), then S meansfor by e that P.

Here is what we shall understand by the Grician Mechanism:

> (GM)   R recognizes S's intention to get R to think that P, and is led by that recognition—through trust in S—to think that P.

GM distinguishes genuine communication from cases in which Source engages in thought control; for example, the case in which I plant incriminating evidence designed to get the police to think you did it. GC and GM differ from Grice's most considered account, but Grice was after what it is to say something and mean something by it, whereas I am mainly after a sufficient condition for communicating something intentionally.

The idea here is that communication is a matter of Source getting a certain thought into Receiver's mind by getting Receiver to recognize that that is what Source is trying to do. On this view, understanding isn't a matter of knowing the semantic properties of the communicative vehicles, it is a matter of recognizing a communicator's intentions.

Language is a conventional means of communication. We can import David Lewis's account of conventions (1969) to show how a convention could emerge between S and R concerning S's utterance. Here is a simple illustration of convention à la Lewis. Suppose you and I are talking on the telephone, and the connection is broken. Assuming we each want to re-establish the connection, what should we do? If we both hang up, and one dials while the other waits, we will succeed. But if we both dial, or both wait, we will fail. Perhaps we fail, or perhaps we succeed by blind luck. Suppose the latter: perhaps I am distracted by a student, and you dial. Now in future if the same thing happens, I may reason as follows: last time, I waited and you dialed. Further, this is the only information bearing on the problem which we share. Hence, doing as I did before (waiting) gives the best available chance of success. It may not be very good, but it is better than acting at random. (If the previous case occurred just 5 minutes ago, it is a pretty good bet.) You reason analogously, and dial. Result: we succeed. After several such successes it will become virtually certain that I will wait while you dial. We have a convention governing this situation. In general, when a group achieves coordination in a certain situation by acting in a certain way, and they act that way because each actor knows, and knows that the others know,[7] that that is how coordination has been achieved in the past, then the group has a convention governing that situation.

As it stands, this analysis applies to cases involving coordination of action, whereas our target involves a kind of coordination between S's action and R's thoughts. But the account is easily generalized, for thinking a thought is, in the relevant sense, something R *does*. It is something R does in the relevant sense because R can have as a reason for adopting the belief that S intends R to believe that P in uttering e the fact that R knows, and knows that S knows, that in the past S's intention in uttering e has been to get R to think that P. If R is then led, through trust in S, to think that P, we have a case which comes to satisfy (GC) because S's utterance of e is governed by a convention existing between S and R. This yields the following account of conventional meaningfor.

> (CM)   Utterance-type E conventionally meansfor (communicates) that P when uttered by S to R if (a) in the past S has uttered tokens of E to R only when S meantfor that P, and (b) this fact is mutually known to S and R, and (c) because of this mutual knowledge it continues to be the case that when S utters tokens of E, S meansfor (communicates) and is understood to meanfor (communicate) that P.[8]

We can now put the preconventional case and the conventional case together in an obvious way. Suppose S intends to get R to believe that a

7. See Bennett's treatment of mutual knowledge (1973 p. 150) for a precise formulation of this epistemic condition.
8. This is a slightly reformulated version of something Bennett claims to borrow from Stephen Schiffer (see Bennett, 1973, p. 152; and Schiffer, 1972).

coconut is about to fall on R, and S goes through a certain performance which results in R recognizing S's intention and, via trust in S, adopting the belief that he is about to be hit on the head by a coconut. Here we have a preconventional case in which communication occurs only because conditions are especially favorable and because S's performance has a certain natural suggestiveness. Next time, however, the mechanism of convention will set it. As repetitions occur, special conditions will no longer be necessary, and S's performance can be streamlined, by a process akin to stimulus substitution, to the point where it need have no natural suggestiveness at all beyond the fact that R and S perceive it as of the same type as its ancestors. The account thus allows for the obvious but theoretically crucial fact that any signal may, as far as its physical characteristics go, have any meaning whatever.

There is a great deal more to be said along these lines before we have anything approaching a complete story. One obvious gap is the lack of any provision for illocutionary forces, that is, for the difference between making statements, asking questions, making requests, issuing warnings, etc.[9] Another concerns the fact that the account as it stands only makes provision for conventions governing the communication of thoughts that P. This is the sort of thing that sentences normally communicate. Evidently, however, there cannot be a separate convention governing the communicative use of each sentence, for there are too many of these. To accomodate the fact that you can't learn a convention for each sentence, communicative conventions have to govern terms, not sentences, and this sorts ill with the Grician proposal which specifies communicative contents in that-clauses. What we need in addition to the idea that linguistic communication produces *thoughts* in Receiver is the idea that it activates *concepts*. Sentences are used to produce thoughts, terms are used to activate concepts. We can simply rewrite GC and GM to apply to the use expressions to activate concepts.

> (GC)   If S (Source) issues (utters, gestures, writes, etc.) e intending thereby to get R (Receiver) to activate the concept C, and relies for the achievement of this upon the Grician Mechanism (GM), then S meansfor C by e.

---

9. The simplest suggestion is to treat every speech act as a complex act of informing the audience of the illocutionary force and expressing the relevant propositional content. What we have so far is a story about expressing propositional contents. You get a reasonable treatment of informing by substituting believing for considering in GC:

> If S (Source) issues (utters, gestures, writes, etc.) e intending thereby to get R (Receiver) to believe *that* P, and relies for the achievement of this upon the Grician Mechanism (GM), then S uses e to inform R *that* P.

(GM)   R recognizes S's intention to get R to activate C, and is led
by that recognition—through trust in S—to activate C.

The clause for conventional meaningfor can evidently be rewritten in the
same way.

It does no good to have communicative conventions governing terms
unless there is some way of computing the conventional meaningfor of a
sentence given its syntax and the conventions governing its terms. Re-
ceivers need to be able to use a sentence as a recipe for combining activated concepts into an occurent thought. We can see how this might
work by riding piggyback on the standard truth-conditional account.
Even though "cat" meansfor CAT and not |cat|, and therefore isn't in a
position to inherit a satisfaction condition from the thing it communicates,
we might yet exploit the machinery of Tarskian semantics to capture the
combinatorics of meaningfor. Concepts are semantically identified, and,
for purposes of articulating the combinatorics that are implicated in linguistic communication, it might be a harmless pretense to treat the
semantic ID of a concept as if it were a semantic content, for example, a
satisfaction condition. With that fiction in place, everything looks to work
more or less as generally supposed: The word gets its satisfaction condition from the concept it meansfor, and the sentence has a truth condition that is a function of the satisfaction conditions of its constituents.
But instead of seeing all this as a specification of the semantic contents of
words (or even concepts), we now see it as a specification of the way the
communicative contents of complex expressions get built out of the communicative contents of their constituents. The combinatorics don't care
whether you are cooking up a thought out of concepts or cooking up
a representation of a proposition from representations of things and
properties. The point of the exercise is to explain how finite learning of
communicative conventions can underwrite a capacity to produce and
understand an unbounded number of signals with distinct communicative
contents.

This account, though sketchy in many ways, at least suggests that it is
possible to imagine a significant role for the application of truth-conditional semantics to natural languages even though one supposes that linguistic expressions are signals rather than representations, and therefore
do not really have satisfaction conditions. Language mastery obviously
calls for some combinatorics. If we want to cleave to the view that terms
meanfor concepts rather than representations, we cannot suppose that
knowing a language is knowing a truth theory for it. But we can suppose
something close. We can suppose that the concepts activated by a complex expression are linked in the process of understanding in a way that
is tracked by the usual truth-conditional combinatorics. Indeed, the only

difference between the standard story and the one urged here is that we don't suppose that sentences are representations whose contents must be duplicated in the head. This loss is sheer gain.

We need not, then, suppose that understanding a language requires knowing what its expressions represent, and we are therefore free to think of language as a set of signals rather than as a set of representations. Rather than a lexicon of expressions with their associated semantic properties (e.g., satisfaction conditions expressed in Mentalese), we have a lexicon of expressions paired with their governing conventions, these being, essentially, instructions for inferring the communicative intentions of their users.

Language and Semantics

It follows from this perspective that languages don't have a semantics, conceived of as Tarski (1944) and Davidson (1967) conceive of semantics. What you need to know about a nonlogical expression is not a satisfaction condition, but its governing convention. Linguistic expressions, being signals, not representations, don't have satisfaction conditions, at least not intrinsically. They have conventional communicative functions. To be a party to a communicative convention, what one needs are the relevant concepts, not Mentalese translations of the word the convention governs. The function of a word is to convey a concept. Although concepts are identified semantically, their semantic IDs, as we saw, are not their representational contents. It follows that words can and do serve their communicative functions without representing at all.[10] Thus, 'elevator' is said to be satisfied by elevators, or to mean the property of being an elevator, because it meansfor ELEVATOR, and ELEVATORs are about elevators. But neither the word, nor the concept, has the property of being an elevator as its representational content. The *word* has no representational content at all; the *concept* has whatever representational content is implicated in having knowledge of elevators, but whatever my knowledge of elevators is, it isn't an |elevator|.

Words, then, are signals, not representations. Signals have communicative functions; representations have semantic contents. When Paul Revere displayed his famous lantern, he signaled that the British were coming by land, but he did not represent that fact. What he did was use a convention-governed signal to communicate a certain message. Had he said, "The British are coming by land," he would also have been using a con-

---

10. I have spoken words in mind here, and phonetically based writing. Ideograms and the like are, perhaps, another matter. It is arguable that, like maps, they communicate what they represent.

vention-governed signal to communicate the same message. The lantern-waving was governed by a temporary convention shared by only a few parties. The sentence is governed by a convention shared by all speakers of English. The sentence no more represents the British route than does displaying the lantern.[11]

There is one further consequence of the present view that should be mentioned before leaving the subject of linguistic communication. Linguistic terms, on the account I favor, communicate concepts. "Cat" meansfor CAT, and "elevator" meansfor ELEVATOR. It follows from this perspective that communication is a matter of degree. Your ELEVATOR probably differs substantially from mine. But even if your ELEVATOR and mine are exactly the same, it may happen that the portion of my ELEVATOR that happens to be implicated in the production of my "elevator" may differ substantially from the portion of your ELEVATOR that my "elevator" happens to activate in you. Communication, then, works best among those who not only share a language but who share a lot of relevant knowledge as well. Indeed, sharing a language requires sharing a lot of knowledge, since understanding a language requires having the concepts conventionally associated with its words, and having the concept is a matter of knowing about the things it applies to. Since learning a given language requires learning the required concepts, those who share a language are bound to share a lot of knowledge.[12]

I think these points help to explain the prevalence of the idea that language is holistic. While it is not true that adding a new primitive changes the meaning of previously existing primitives, it is true that understanding 'cat' requires having a CAT, and that involves a great deal more than simply having a |cat| in the representational repertoire. To have a CAT, one has to have a FOOT and a FUR and an ANIMAL and so on. And each of these will require other concepts in turn. It is obvious that if you confuse representations and concepts, you can quickly turn these otherwise harmless facts into an argument for holism: To understand 'cat', you have to have a CAT. To have a CAT, you have to have an ANIMAL. But if CATs are |cat|s, and ANIMALs are |animal|s, then understanding 'cat' requires having an |animal|, and we are off to the races. Being a concept is a holistic property in the sense of Fodor and Lepore (1992): To have one, you have to have lots. But it doesn't follow from this that to understand one word, you have to to understand lots, nor does it follow

11. Certain formalisms—artificial languages, as they are sometimes called—are like maps and graphs in exploiting a link between the representational content of complex expressions and their communicative content. See Swoyer (1991) for a treatment of this point.
12. This has a misleadingly Whorfian sound. But Whorf (1956) held that what you can know is a function of what you can say. I hold only that what you do know is, to some extent, a result of acquiring the languages you speak.

that adding a primitive expression changes the meanings of previously existing primitives. This is surely good news for language learners.

Language, Representation, and Thought

I have been urging the idea that there is a very large gap between language and mental representation. Words are signals, not representations, so,

1. The word 'cat' doesn't represent cats.

The word 'cat' meansfor (but doesn't mean) CAT. CATs are knowledge structures, structures of attitudes. Though concepts are semantically identified, their IDs are not their contents. So,

2. The thing 'cat' communicates, namely a CAT, doesn't represent cats either.

Since CATs are attitude structures, and since one can have attitudes about cats without representing cats, it follows that,

3. It is possible, in principle, to understand 'cat' even if you don't have a |cat| in your representational repertoire.

To put the point a bit differently, you cannot read off what you can represent from what linguistic expressions you can understand because

1. Which linguistic expressions you can understand depends on what you know.
2. Knowing things is a matter of having attitudes.
3. Attitudes are not representations: Although every attitude involves representation, you cannot identify representational content with attitude content without squeezing targets (and hence representational error) out of the picture.

This opens up the possibility that you can say and understand things you cannot represent, as well as the possibility that you can represent things you cannot say. How much of a gap there really is here is an empirical issue that depends on what basic intenders and representations we actually come equipped with. The gap may be very small, or it may be rather large. I want to explore the possibility that it is rather large, not because I think it is rather large, but because I think it is revealing to ask what it would take to accommodate a large gap.

Suppose, then, that you actually can and do have concepts of a lot of things you cannot represent, that is, that for a significant number of choices for X, you have organized knowledge about Xs but cannot represent the property of being an X. And let's add to this the possibility emphasized by Burge (1979) and Putnam (1975) that you can be said to have a concept of X even though most of the relevant knowledge is in the heads of experts to whom you are prepared to defer, including nonhuman experts such as encyclopedias. Finally, let's add Gregory's idea (1970) that a lot of the knowledge we can properly be said to have is in our technology: we know how to prepare a camera-ready manuscript because we know how to use a word processor, and we know how to open a can because we know how to use a can opener.[13] Then we can have lots of concepts of things we cannot (or need not, or do not) represent, either because, in general, you can have knowledge of Xs in you head without representing Xs, or because a lot of the requisite knowledge isn't in your head anyway, but in someone else's head, or in a book, or in the design of a machine or an institution.

All of this opens a gap between words and representations because you can be said to understand the word when you can be said to have the associated concept, but you can have the associated concept without being able to represent whatever it is a concept *of*. To accommodate this gap, we need a pair of distinctions.

- We need to distinguish the knowledge you have from the knowledge that is in your head. Your *m*-knowledge—'*m*' for 'mental', the knowledge in your head—is a proper part of your *c*-knowledge—'*c*' for 'culture', the knowledge you have in virtue of being party to a certain culture. Corresponding to this distinction is a distinction between *m*-concepts and *c*-concepts, and *m*-thoughts and *c*-thoughts. The point to be made is that you can *c*-conceive and *c*-think a lot of things you cannot *m*-conceive and *m*-think.
- We need to distinguish what you can think and conceive from what you can represent.

I think all of this is good news, for it gives us elbow room for dealing with a troubling problem about concept acquisition. In Fodor (1975) we have an argument to the effect that we cannot acquire any new primitive concepts by learning (as opposed to evolution, serendipitous trauma, maturation, and the like). As originally formulated, the argument is directed at the Piagetian hypothesis that (1) different developmental stages are characterized by different representational power, and (2) that stage transition is mediated by learning.

It might really turn out that the kinds of representational system that children use is, in a principled sense, weaker than the kind of

13. If we think of encyclopedias and the maintenance or experts (certifying them and the like) as bits of cultural technology, then the Burge-Putnam point becomes a special case of Gregory's point.

system that adults use, and that a reasonable account of the stages of cognitive development could be elaborated by referring to increases in the expressive power of such systems. What I think one *cannot* have, however, is that concept learning provides the mechanisms for the stage-to-stage transitions. That is, if the child's cognitive development is fundamentally the development of increasingly powerful representational/conceptual systems, then cognitive development cannot be the consequence of concept learning. (Fodor, 1975, p. 89)

I quote the argument Fodor gave for this conclusion at length for reasons that will become clear in a moment.

Suppose, e.g., that your are a stage one child trying to learn the concept C. Well, the least you have to do is to learn the conditions under which something is an instance of (falls under) C. So, presumably, you have to learn something of the form $(x)(x$ is C iff x is $F)$ where F is some concept that applies whenever C does. Clearly, however, a necessary condition on being able to learn *that* is that one's conceptual system should contain F. So now consider the case where C is, as it were, a stage two concept. If something is a stage two concept, then it must follow that it is not coextensive with any stage *one* concept; otherwise, the difference between stages wouldn't be a difference in the expressive power of the conceptual systems that characterize the stages. But if the stage one child can't represent the extension of C in terms of some concept in the system available to him, he can't represent it at all since, by definition, his conceptual system just *is* the totality of representational devices that he can use for cognitive processing. And if he can't *represent* the extension of C, then he can't *learn* C since, by hypothesis, concept learning involves projecting and confirming biconditionals which determine the extension of the concept being learned. So, either the conditions on applying a stage two concept *can* be represented in terms of some stage one concept, in which case there is no obvious sense in which the stage two conceptual system is more powerful than the stage one conceptual system, or there are stage two concepts whose extension *cannot* be represented in the stage one vocabulary, in which case there is no way for the stage one child to learn them. (p. 90)

The argument is an embarrassment to Piagetians, as Fodor pointed out, because they suppose that children move through developmental stages that require ever-richer representational resources, and the argument shows that you cannot increase your representational power by learning. Since Piagetians have no other mechanism up their sleeves, they must fall back on maturation. But the stages in question look far too content-dependent to be the effects of general brain maturation. Fodor takes this fight from Piaget by a knockout.

But it isn't only Piaget who is embarrassed. What are we to say about the obvious fact that our conceptual resources are much richer than Aristotle's? Aristotle didn't have the concept of a quark, for example, or of a gene. Evolution, maturation, and the like are not options here. We could hold that the troublesome concepts are complex, and that all we have over Aristotle is that we put things together in ways he didn't. But if we think of this as simply a matter of representational combinatorics, we will have to exhibit them, that is, define the property of being a quark in terms of properties that Aristotle had at his representational fingertips. Good luck.

Not to worry, however. We are now in a position to see that the argument confuses concepts with representations. (That's why I wanted the full quotation in front of us.) What Fodor has given us is an argument that primitive *representations* cannot be learned, that is, that one's basic representational power cannot be altered by learning. With this I am in complete agreement: One's representational repertoire is part of one's innate architecture. But, of course, concepts are not representations, but knowledge structures, and these are acquired and altered by learning. One can acquire the concept of a quark, that is, an organized body of knowledge about quarks, without altering one's representational capacities at all. I have concepts Aristotle did not have, and could not have formulated, because I know a great deal more physics than Aristotle did. Both my *m*-concepts and *c*-concepts vastly outrun his simply because I am part of a culture whose scientific and technological resources vastly outrun those of ancient Greece. You don't need to increase your representational power to increase your conceptual power. Stage two children arguably differ from stage one children in conceptual power, just as we differ from Aristotle in conceptual power. But there is no compelling reason to suppose that any of us differ in representational power.[14]

Once again, it is the practice of identifying concepts semantically, in terms of what they are knowledge *about*, that is at the root of the confusion. We can speak both of representations *of quarks* and of concepts *of quarks*, and this tempts us to think of concepts as representations. Faced

14. One sometimes hears connectionists saying that connectionist networks learn new representations (e.g., Clark, 1989). Again, this is a confusion. The representational resources of a network consist of the set of possible activation vectors and the set of points in its weight space. These, evidently, do not change as a function of learning. What does change is which point in weight space the network occupies at a time, and, as a consequence, which activation vectors actually occur. This might model concept learning, since it is plausible to think of changes in weights as changes in stored knowledge (Cummins, 1994).

with Fodor's argument that representational power cannot be increased by learning, we think we are faced with the result that one's conceptual power cannot be increased by learning, and this seems to fly in the face of both the developmental changes and the obvious intellectual advances of culture in general, and science in particular. The paradox evaporates when we realize that having a concept of a quark is not having something with the property of being a quark as its representational content, but rather having organized knowledge of quarks.

There is another route to the conclusion that you cannot have a QUARK unless you also have a |quark|. According to the Representational Theory of Attitude Content, having an attitude with the content that quarks are constituents of hadrons requires having a representation with the content that quarks are constituents of hadrons. According to the Language of Thought hypothesis (LOT), having a representation with the content that quarks are constituents of hadrons is having a mental sentence that means that quarks are constituents of hadrons. Since having the sentence requires having the terms in it, and since 'quark' is a term in 'Quarks are constituents of hadrons', it looks like you have to have a |quark| in your language of thought if you are going to have knowledge of quarks. No term, no sentence; no sentence, no knowledge; no knowledge, no concept.

You can take your pick about where to abort this trip. You can deny RTAC, as I do, on the grounds that it forces one to identify the content of an attitude with the content of its constituent representation, leaving no room for the target-content distinction and hence no room for representational error. Or you can deny LOT, as I also do, on the grounds that the arbitrariness of its primitives inevitably leads to a use theory of content, and from there, once again, to the conclusion that there is no representational error. It is a comfort to me that LOT and RATC together lead to the silly conclusion that Aristotle and Einstein cannot differ in conceptual power.

References

Armstrong, D. 1968. *The Materialist Theory of Mind*. London: Routledge & Kegan Paul.

Bennett, J. 1973. "The Meaning-Nominalist Strategy." *Foundations of Language*. 10:141–168.

Bennett, J. 1976. *Linguistic Behavior*. Cambridge: Cambridge University Press.

Block, N. 1986. "Advertisement for a Semantics for Psychology." In P. French, T. Uehling, Jr., and H. Wettstein, eds. *Studies in the Philosophy of Mind*, Vol. 10, *Midwest Studies in Philosophy*. Minneapolis: University of Minnesota Press.

Braine, M. D. S. 1978. "On the Relation Between the Natural Logic of Reasoning and Standard Logic." In G. H. Bower, ed. *Psychological Review*. 85:1–21.

Burge, T. 1979. "Individualism and the Mental." *Midwest Studies in Philosophy*. 4:73–121.

Carey, S. 1985. *Conceptual Change in Childhood*. Cambridge, Mass.: MIT Press.

Chomsky, N. 1959. "Review of Skinner's Verbal Behavior." *Language* 35:26–58.

Clark, A. 1989. *Microcognition: Philosophy, Cognitive Science, and Parallel Distributed Processing*. Cambridge, Mass.: MIT Press. A Bradford Book.

Cummins, D. 1988. "The Role of Understanding in Solving Word Problems." *Cognitive Psychology* 20:405–438.

Cummins, D. 1991. "Children's Interpretations of Arithmetic Word Problems." *Cognition and Instruction* 8:261–289.

Cummins, R. 1979. "Intention, Meaning and Truth Conditions." *Philosophical Studies* 35:345–360.

Cummins, R. 1983. *The Nature of Psychological Explanation*. Cambridge, Mass.: MIT Press. A Bradford Book.

Cummins, R. 1984. "Functional Analysis." In E. Sober, ed. *Conceptual Issues in Evolutionary Biology: An Anthology*. Cambridge, Mass.: MIT Press. A Bradford Book.

Cummins, R. 1989. *Meaning and Mental Representation*. Cambridge, Mass.: MIT Press. A Bradford Book.

Cummins, R. 1991a. "Methodological Reflections on Belief." In R. Bogdan, ed. *Mind and Common Sense*. Cambridge: Cambridge University Press.

Cummins, R. 1991b. "Form, Interpretation, and the Uniqueness of Content: Response to Morris." *Minds and Machines* 1:31–42.

Cummins, R. 1992. "Conceptual role semantics and the explanatory role of content." *Philosophical Studies* 65:103–127.

Cummins, R. 1994. "Connectionism and the Rationale Constraint on Cognitive Explanation." *Philosophical Perspectives*

Davidson, D. 1967. "Truth and Meaning." *Synthese* 17:304–323.

Davidson, D. 1973. "The Material Mind." In P. Suppes, ed. *Logic, Methodology and Philosophy of Science IV*. Amsterdam: North-Holland Publishing Company.

Dennett, D. 1986. "The Logical Geography of Computational Approaches: A View from the East Pole." In R. Harnish and M. Brand, eds. *The Representation of Knowledge and Belief*. Tucson: University of Arizona Press.

Dennett, D. 1987. *The Intentional Stance.* Cambridge, Mass.: MIT Press. A Bradford Book.

Dretske, F. 1981. *Knowledge and the Flow of Information.* Cambridge, Mass.: MIT Press. A Bradford Book.

Dretske, F. 1986. "Misrepresentation." In R. Bodgan ed. *Belief.* Oxford: Oxford University Press.

Fodor, J. 1975. *The Language of Thought.* New York: Crowell.

Fodor, J. 1980. "Methodological Solipsism Considered as a Research Strategy in Cognitive Science." *Behavioral and Brain Sciences* 3:63–109.

Fodor, J. 1982. "Cognitive Science and the Twin Earth Problem." *Notre Dame Journal of Formal Logic.* 23:98–119.

Fodor, J. 1983. *The Modularity of Mind: An Essay on Faculty Psychology.* Cambridge, Mass.: MIT Press. A Bradford Book.

Fodor, J. 1987. *Psychosemantics: The Problem of Meaning in the Philosophy of Mind.* Cambridge, Mass.: MIT Press. A Bradford Book.

Fodor, J. 1990a. "Psychosemantics, or Where do Truth Conditions Come From." In W. Lycan ed. *Mind and Cognition.* Oxford: Basil Blackwell pp. 312–338.

Fodor, J. 1990b. *A Theory of Content and Other Essays.* Cambridge, Mass.: MIT Press. A Bradford Book.

Fodor, J. 1994. *The Elm and the Expert.* Cambridge, Mass.: MIT Press. A Bradford Book.

Fodor, J., Bever, T., and Garrett, M. 1974. *The Psychology of Language.* New York: McGraw-Hill Book Co.

Fodor, J., and Lepore, E. 1992. *Holism: A Shopper's Guide.* Oxford: Basil Blackwell.

Fodor, J., and McLaughlin, B. 1990. "Connectionism and the Problem of Systematicity: Why Smolensky's Solution Doesn't Work." *Cognition.* 35:183–204.

Fodor, J., and Pylyshyn, Z. 1988. "Connectionism and Cognitive Architecture: A Critical Analysis." *Cognition* 28:3–71.

Gregory, R. 1970. *The Intelligent Eye.* New York: McGraw-Hill Book Co.

Grice, H. P. 1957. "Meaning." *Philosophical Review* 66:377–388.

Grice, H. P. 1975. "Logic and Conversation." In P. Cole, and J. Morgan, eds. *Syntax and Semantics,* Vol 3. London, Academic Press.

Harnad, S. 1990. "The Symbol Grounding Problem." *Physica D,* 42:335–346.

Haugeland, J. 1985. *Artificial Intelligence. The Very Idea.* Cambridge, Mass.: MIT Press. A Bradford Book.

Haugeland, J. 1990. "Representational Genera." In W. Ramsey, S. Stich, and D. Rumelhart, eds. *Philosophy and Connectionist Theory.* Hillsdale, N.J.: Lawrence Erlbaum Associates.

Hempel, C. 1950. "Problems and Changes in the Empiricist Criterion of Meaning." *Review Internationale de Philosophie* 11:41–63.

Hubel, D. H., and Wiesel, T. N., 1979. "Brain Mechanisms of Vision." In *The Brain: A Scientific American Book.* New York: W. H. Freeman.

Lewis, D. 1969. *Convention: A Philosophical Study.* Cambridge, Mass.: Harvard University Press.

Loui, R. 1991. "Ampliative Inference, Computation, and Dialectic." In R. Cummins and J. Pollock, eds. *Philosophy and AI: Essays at the Interface.* Cambridge, Mass.: MIT Press. A Bradford Book.

Marr, D. 1982. *Vision.* New York: W. H. Freeman.

Miller, G. 1956. "Magical Number 7 ± 2: Some Limits on Our Capacity for Processing Information." *Psychological Review* 63 8:1–97.

Millikan, R. 1984. *Language, Thought, and Other Biological Categories.* Cambridge, Mass.: MIT Press. A Bradford Book.

Neisser, U. 1981. "John Dean's Memory." *Cognition* 9:1–22.

Pallas, S. L., Roe, A. W., and Sur. M. 1990. "Visual Projections Induced into the Auditory Pathway of Ferrets. I. Novel Inputs to Primary Auditory Cortex (AI) from the LP/

Pulvinar Complex and the Topography of the MGN—AI Projection." *Journal of Comparative Neurology* 1:50.

Papineau, D. 1987. *Reality and Representation*. Oxford: Basil Blackwell.

Perlman, M. 1993. *Conceptual Flux: The Case against Misrepresentation*, dissertation thesis, University of Arizona, Tucson.

Pollock, J. 1986. *Contemporary Theories of Knowledge*. Totowa, N.J.: Rowman and Littlefield.

Pollock, J. 1989. *How to Build a Person: A Prolegomenon*. Cambridge, Mass.: MIT Press. A Bradford Book.

Putnam, H. 1975. "The Meaning of 'Meaning'." In K. Gunderson, ed. *Language, Mind and Knowledge*. Minnesota Studies in Philosophy of Science Series, Vol. 7.

Pylyshyn, Z. 1984. *Computation and Cognition*. Cambridge, Mass.: MIT Press. A Bradford Book.

Quine, W. V. O. 1953. "Two Dogmas of Empiricism." In *From a Logical Point of View and Other Essays*. New York: Harper & Row.

Quine, W. V. O. 1960. *Word and Object*. Cambridge, Mass.: MIT Press.

Rips, L. J. 1983. "Cognitive Processes in Propositional Reasoning." *Psychological Review*. 90:38–71.

Schiffer, S. 1972. *Meaning*. Oxford: Oxford University Press.

Schiffer, S. 1987. *Remnants of Meaning*. Cambridge, Mass.: MIT Press. A Bradford Book.

Schwarz, G. 1992. "Connectionism, Processing, Memory." *Connection Science* 4:207–226.

Searle, J. 1980. "Minds, Brains, and Programs." *Behavioral and Brain Sciences* 3:417–424.

Smith, E. E., and Medin, D., 1981. *Categories and Concepts*. Cambridge, Mass.: Harvard University Press.

Smolensky, P. 1987. "The Constituent Structure of Connectionist Mental States: A Reply to Fodor and Pylyshyn." *Southern Journal of Philosophy*. 26 (Suppl.):137–163.

Smolensky, P. 1994. "Constituent Structure and Explanation in an Integrated Connectionist/Symbolic Cognitive Architecture." In C. Macdonald and G. Macdonald, eds. *The Philosophy of Psychology: Debates on Psychological Explanation*. Oxford: Basil Blackwell.

Smolensky, P., Legendre, G., and Miyata, Y. 1992. "Principles for an Integrated Connectionist/Symbolic Theory of Higher Cognition." Technical Report CU-CS-600-92. Department of Computer Science, University of Colorado at Boulder.

Spelke, E. 1990. "The Origins of Physical Knowledge." In L. Weiskrantz, ed. *Thought Without Language*. Oxford: Oxford University Press.

Stampe, D. 1977. "Towards a Causal Theory of Linguistic Representation." In P. French, T. Uehling, and H. Wettstein eds. *Midwest Studies in Philosophy*. Minneapolis: University of Minnesota Press, pp. 42–63.

Stich, S. 1983. *From Folk Psychology to Cognitive Science: The Case Against Belief*. Cambridge, Mass.: MIT Press. A Bradford Book.

Sur, M., Garraghty, P. E., and Roe, A. W. 1988. "Experimentally Induced Visual Projections into Auditory Thalamus and Cortex." *Science* 242:1437.

Sur, M. Pallas, S. L., and Roe, A. W. 1990. "Cross Modal Plasticity in Cortical Development: Differentiation and Specification of Sensory Neocortex." *Trends in Neuroscience* 13:227.

Swoyer, C. 1991. "Structural Representation and Surrogative Reasoning." *Synthese* 87:449–508.

Tarski, A. 1944. "The Semantic Conception of Truth." *Philosophy and Phenomenological Research*. 4.

Tolman, E. C 1948. "Cognitive Maps in Rats and Men." *Psychological Review*. 55:189–208.

Whorf, B. L. 1956. "Science and Linguistics." In J. B. Carroll, ed. *Language, Thought, and Reality: Selected Writings of Benjamin Lee Whorf*. Cambridge, Mass.: MIT Press.

Wynn, K. 1992. "Addition and Subtraction by Human Infants." *Nature* 358:749–750.

Index